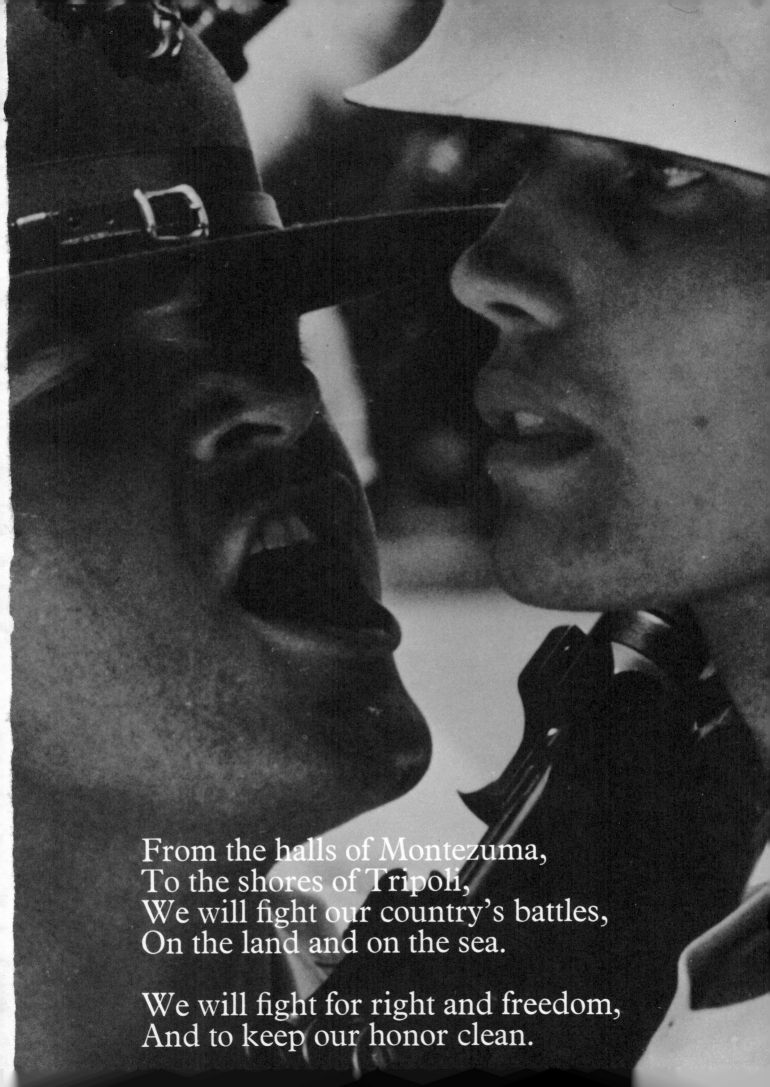

From the halls of Montezuma,
To the shores of Tripoli,
We will fight our country's battles,
On the land and on the sea.

We will fight for right and freedom,
And to keep our honor clean.

We are proud to bear the title of

UNITED STATES MARINES

THOMAS A. SIEFRING

CHARTWELL BOOKS INC.

A BISON BOOK

Published by
Chartwell Books Inc.,
A Division of Book Sales Inc.,
110 Enterprise Avenue
Secaucus, New Jersey 07094

© Copyright 1979 Bison Books Limited

Produced by
Bison Books Limited
4 Cromwell Place
London SW7

ISBN: 0 89009 272 9

Library of Congress Catalog Number:
78 74053

Printed in Hong Kong

CONTENTS

INTRODUCTION

The Marine Corps was not fully prepared for its greatest mission on 7 December 1941. Experience was needed and that was only gained in combat; such amphibious landings as Guadalcanal and Tarawa were far from model landings. But once a technique was learned by the Marines they never forgot it, and they did learn from experience. The history of World War II in the Pacific can largely be written in terms of such Army landings as at Kwajalein and Ie Shima, or the Marine landings at Saipan, Peleliu and Iwo Jima. The US victories in North Africa and Europe were made possible by US Army landings, but the most important thing to remember is that those Army landings were based upon Fleet Marine Force doctrine. In fact four US Army divisions were specially trained by the Marines in amphibious tactics and took a major part in these operations:

1st Infantry Division
   Oran, Sicily and Normandy
3rd Infantry Division
   Casablanca, Sicily and Anzio
7th Infantry Division
   Attu, Kiska, Kwajalein, Leyte and Okinawa
9th Infantry Division
   Port Lyautey, Sicily and Normandy

Just as the amphibious landing was at the heart of Marine Corps Doctrine, so was the role of the helicopter in the Korean War. It is extremely hard to analyze Korea and Vietnam in a truly objective fashion, but there can be no doubt that the single most important tactical innovation was the use of the helicopter. Numerous Marine Corps Helicopter units served throughout the Korean War and served with distinction. Without the helicopter literally thousands of Marines would have died before being evacuated to adequate medical facilities. Also the helicopter brought much needed supplies, food, ammunitions and all manner of equipment without which the front-line Marines would have been in dire straits. The continued development of the helicopter after the Korean War and up to the Vietnam War saw an extension of its potential. Major battles and campaigns were being supported by helicopter gunships, observation helicopters, and even more important cargo helicopters and evacuation choppers that took the wounded from under the guns of the enemy to safety. This machine is now as much a part of Marine Corps philosophy as the amphibious landings, and is here to stay. In the words of an ex-Commandant of the Marine Corps, General Lemuel Shepherd, after the Inchon-Seoul amphibious operation in 1950:

No effort should be spared to get helicopters . . . helicopters in any form, to the theater at once, and on a priority higher than any other weapon.

Right: *Recruits undergoing basic training at Quantico, Virginia in 1971.*
Far right: *A mud-covered recruit completes a course at Parris Island, 1971.*
Below: *Marines demonstrate amphibious landings to civilians.*

Under the command of Marine Captain Samuel Nicholas 230 Marines and 50 seamen landed on the island of New Providence to aid Washington's army, 3 March 1776. This was the second painting in a series depicting the moment the Continental Marines stepped ashore from ships of the Continental fleet commanded by Commodore Esek Hopkins. The artist was Major Charles Waterhouse.

The Green Coats

That two Battalions of Marines be raised consisting of one Colonel, two Lieutenant Colonels, two Majors & Officers as usual in other regiments, that they consist of an equal number of privates with other battalions; that particular care be taken that no person be appointed to office or enlisted into said Battalions, but such as are good seamen, or so acquainted with maritime affairs as to be able to serve to advantage by sea. . . .

Resolution of the Continental Congress creating the US Marine Corps on 10 November 1775.

The history of the United States Marine Corps started on a bleak November day in 1775. The story began when the fledgling Continental Navy prepared for its first crack at the mighty British Fleet. This was a time of crisis when all ties were sundered with the mother country, something which the colonists were divided about. It was about seven months after the Battles of Lexington and Concord and young Americans were getting ready to defend their homes and beliefs, when the sloop *Katy* docked at Philadelphia. The first man ashore was Mr John Trevett, a native of Rhode Island, who came from a seafaring family. He was destined to become one of the very first men to serve as an American Marine.

On 28 November 1775 Congress commissioned the first Marine officer, Captain Samuel Nicholas, a blacksmith's son, and the United States Marine Corps was born. Commodore Esek Hopkins, another Rhode Islander, was appointed Commander in Chief of the fleet, which consisted of only eight ships, not quite a squadron and hardly a fleet. Hopkins was a calculating and shrewd individual; while his ships were trapped in the ice of Delaware Bay, he trained his 234 men to act as Marines. Captain Nicholas, the senior Marine officer, was on board the flagship, the 24-gun *Alfred*, with Lieutenants John Fitzpatrick and Matthew Parke. Another individual who was to rise to great fame with the Navy also served on board, John Paul Jones. The 1st Lieutenant Trevett was serving on the 20-gun *Columbus*.

On 17 February 1776 the ice melted and the small fleet sailed to its destiny. Hopkins had his orders which were to engage the British ships-of-the-line off

Marines under the command of Captain John Trevett captured and held New Providence again in January 1778. "Flag Raising at New Providence" by Major Charles Waterhouse recreates the moment when the 13 Stars and Stripes was raised over the island's main fort.

the Carolina and Virginia coasts. He decided to throw caution to the wind and attempt something original. He knew that Washington was extremely short of gunpowder, so he planned a daring raid on the British supply depot in the Bahamas. The 1 March saw the small American fleet rendezvous off Great Abaco Island in the Bahamas. A landing party was organized: a Marine detachment under Captain Nicholas and 50 sailors under Lieutenant Thomas Weaver of the *Cabot*. They were ordered to set sail in the 12-gun *Providence*, accompanied by two captured sloops, for Nassau on the island

Above: *"Assault at Penobscot" by Waterhouse recreates the Marine attack up the peninsula's western face led by Captain John Walsh in 1779.*
Below: *Originally captured from the English by the French, the HMS* Sandwich *is here taken from the French by Captain Daniel Carmick and the Marine Detachment of the USF* Constitution *on 11 May 1800 in Puerta Plata, Santo Domingo. The painting is by R A Salmon.*

of New Providence, where 600 barrels of black gunpowder were stored. This first American Expeditionary Force, because that in essence was what it was, attempted to surprise the British garrison, but luck was against them. The small landing force was spotted and the fort fired an alarm signal. The Marines landed without opposition for the very first time on Sunday, 3 March 1776, two miles east of Fort Montagu. Fort Montagu surrendered soon after and at sunrise, Nicholas marched on the town, where he demanded the keys to Fort Nassau, which were promptly turned over and the British colors taken down. The entire operation had been a success up to that point. Little did Hopkins and Nicholas know that the wily Governor Montfont Browne had dispatched the majority of the gunpowder supplies, 162 barrels, to Florida. With the Marines in possession of the defenses, Commodore Hopkins sailed the *Alfred* into Nassau harbor and himself came ashore. Trevett was ordered to take a detachment of Marines and place the governor under house arrest until the fleet was ready to sail. The Bahamas landings resulted in the capture of only 24 barrels of gunpowder; however 46 heavy cannon were taken from Fort Nassau and 12 small cannons and 15 mortars from Fort Montagu. The fleet set sail with their booty and took Governor Browne and two other officials as well. The return journey was uneventful until Block Island was reached where the lone British frigate

Glasgow engaged the brig *Cabot*. It was courageous for the British frigate to fight the entire American "fleet"; the engagement raged for over one hour and a half. Eleven Americans died as a result, including three Marines from the *Cabot*, 2nd Lieutenant John H Wilson and 2nd Lieutenant Fitzpatrick of the *Alfred*. The expedition stirred so much excitement in the Colonies that the president of the Continental Congress, John Hancock, personally congratulated Commodore Hopkins on his unqualified success.

Americans during the Revolutionary War served as Marines in the individual navies of the various states and even on privateers. Congress never really organized the Marines, mainly because of the scarcity of men and vessels. Nonetheless on 25 June 1776 Congress created Samuel Nicholas Major of Marines, the highest post held during the war. He was directed to raise four companies of Marines for the Continental frigates then being built. However the Board of Admiralty stipulated that the major of Marines should serve at sea and only on a ship-of-the-line, which the United States Navy did not possess during the entire conflict. Therefore Major Nicholas was forced to serve on land, chained to a desk. He never went to sea again as a Marine but he did fight on land with George Washington at Trenton and Princeton.

The uniform of a Marine was decided by Congress on 5 September 1776. Officers were to wear:

A Green Coat faced with white, Round Cuffs, Slash'd Sleeves and Pockets; with Buttons round the Cuff, Silver Epaulett on the right shoulder – Skirts turn'd back, Buttons to suit the Faceing. White waistcoat and Breeches edged with Green, Black Gaiters & Garters.

Enlisted men were to wear green shirts, "if and when they could be procured." Green was to become the distinctive color of the Marines. The total number of Marines who served during the Revolutionary War were as figures show:

1   Major
30   Captains
100 Lieutenants
2000 Enlisted men

Before the end of 1776 the Continental Marines fought in their first land campaign. Washington's army had been driven off Long Island, through Manhattan, White Plains and up to Peekshill, and was now being pursued across New Jersey. Philadelphia was threatened by the advancing British, and the Marines on the ships in the Delaware were ordered to aid the army in holding up the British, if not stopping them outright. Major Nicholas received orders to form a battalion of 131 men from the existing Marine companies assigned to the frigates under construction at Philadelphia. These companies were under Captains Benjamin Dean, Robert

"Defeat on Lake Champlain" depicts the Marines jumping overboard to prevent Benedict Arnold from scuttling his ships, 13 October 1776.

Mullan and Andrew Porter. The fourth company under Captain Samuel Shaw did not join this force because their ship, the frigate *Randolph*, was preparing to set sail. On 2 December 1776 Nicholas' Marines were ordered to join up with Colonel John Cadwalader's volunteers. Congress evacuated to Baltimore and Washington, tired of his constant retreat, turned on the British when they least expected it. He decided to cross the Delaware on Christmas night and attack the Hessian troops holding Trenton. Brigadier General Ewing was ordered to cross the river below Trenton and seal off the possible escape route of the Hessians. Cadwalader's division, consisting of some 1800 men, was to cross at Bristol, Pennsylvania and create a diversion of sorts to draw off any enemy troops in that area. Meanwhile Washington would attack the main Hessian force from the north. Washington's battle-weary men crossed the Delaware and made their famous march, the majority without shoes and adequate clothing to protect them from the cold winter wind. They managed it, and completely surprised the entire garrison, killing 22, wounding 92 and capturing 948, with only four Americans losing their lives in the attack. Washington, although victorious, had to retreat across the river once again because Ewing and Cadwalader did not manage to make a crossing.

Undeterred, Washington planned another attack against the unsuspecting British. He crossed the Delaware once again and marched straight into Trenton. Major General Cornwallis proceeded rapidly with 8000 troops to crush him once and for all. To gain

time Washington sent Colonel Edward Hand to delay the British as long as he could. Hand fought a delaying action at Maidenhead, northeast of Trenton, and at the action of Assunpink Creek the Marines were a vital part of the advance force. Washington then circled around Cornwallis' left flank and made for Princeton. He detached Brigadier General Hugh Mercer's brigade and Cadwalader's volunteers to hold the stone bridge two miles south of Princeton on the main Princeton-Trenton road. But as Mercer's advance force emerged from the nearby woods, they ran into two British regiments commanded by Lieutenant Colonel Charles Mawhood. The 17th British Regiment fired on the surprised Americans and then charged with bayonets. Brigadier General Mercer was killed and the American force initially retreated. Then Cadwalader's force marched out of the wood and opened fire on the British, his marines and soldiers making a determined stand on the right flank. Washington rallied the Americans and they held their positions. Then reinforcements arrived and the face of the battle was reversed. Mawhood was forced to retreat with his 17th Regiment to Trenton while the 55th British Regiment retreated to Princeton where it subsequently surrendered. The entire action only took 20 minutes, with the British casualties numbering 273 men and the Americans losing 40 killed and 100 wounded. Thus ended the first phase of Marine commitment to their initial land campaign.

The Continental Marines were asked to participate in one more amphibious landing before the close of the Revolution. This second landing was on the coast of Maine and was in the face of enemy fire. In June 1779 General Sir Henry Clinton, commander of all British troops in

America, ordered a fort to be built at the mouth of the Penobscot River. The Americans were quick to take up the challenge and a strong expeditionary force, the Massachusetts militia, was prepared under Brigadier General Solomon Lovell to destroy the fort. In the afternoon, 25 July 1779, the American force arrived off the Penobscot. The British commander Brigadier General MacLean knew about their approach for at least four days in advance and so speeded up work on the fortifications. On 26 July the British and American warships fought a two-hour battle, resulting in the British withdrawing up the river. Then the Marines from *Providence* under Captain John Welsh landed on Nautilus Island, which gave them complete command of the harbor. An 18-pound and 12-pound cannon were set up on the island and the fire from these two batteries succeeded in driving the British ships even further up river. In a dawn attack Captain Welsh and his Marines assaulted the mainland peninsula where the British were constructing their fortifications. The Marines were on the right and the other two divisions holding the center and left respectively. The strongest British positions were on the right and the Marines succeeded in forcing the British regulars back into the fort. Meanwhile the British squadron from New York, commanded by Sir George Collier, appeared off the Penobscot on 13 August. The Americans were so shaken that they withdrew back on board ship and set sail up the river, fleeing from the British squadron who immediately pursued them. The result was that Captain Saltonstall, the naval commander, ran his ships aground and set fire to them except for three which were captured by the British. This entire operation was a fiasco from the very beginning – the only heroic part was that played by the Marines in driving the British back into their fort.

The Marines fought in numerous single naval duels throughout the Revolutionary War. The American Marines in the Revolution were a mixture of amateurs, seafarers and heroes. They were men of feeling who fought for their beliefs and rights as free men. They did their duty although surrounded by incompetents on all sides. Their history was just beginning and they were on a long road to glory.

After the Revolution the nation's military forces were disbanded. Ten years after the last Continental Marine had been discharged realistic thinking prevailed. The decision-makers realized that a nation, young and defenseless was an easy target for a bully. In the next 30 years the United States fought against the Barbary

Pirates, France and finally the old enemy England. The main cause of the next three wars was the seizure of merchant ships and sailors. This led to the eventual conflict with England in 1812. On 27 March 1794 Congress ordered that six naval frigates be built and the enlistment of an adequate number of seamen and Marines to man them. Originally they were intended to fight the Barbary Pirates, but they were also to protect US shipping, ports and seamen from France and England.

It was not until 11 July 1798 that a Congressional act actually established a Marine Corps, and the Corps was born. This act provided for 881 men: 1 major, 4 captains, 16 first lieutenants, 12 second lieutenants, 48 sergeants, 48 corporals, 32 drummers and 720 privates. All enlistments were for three years, and the US Senate would appoint all officers to the Corps. From the very beginning the primary principle was that a Marine is a fighter first and a specialist second. Discipline was tough; in fact the Corps was directly modelled on the British Navy. Punishment was severe: an offender could be flogged, have his head shaved, be assigned to hard labor or forfeit his rum.

The uniforms were elaborate and fancy. An officer wore a long blue coat

"Mustering Out" recalls the last Continental Marines to see service in the Revolution, 1 April 1783.

with red lapels and lining, a red vest and blue breeches. The jacket had numerous buttons bearing a rope-entwined anchor and the American eagle. Epaulets denoted rank. The enlisted men wore a blue coat and trousers trimmed with red, a cocked hat, and a black leather collar that kept their heads erect at all times. This collar gave them the everlasting name of "Leathernecks."

The first official leader of the Corps was William Burrows, a native of South Carolina and a well-established lawyer. He set up the Marine Head-

"John Adams Reviews Jones' Marines." This contingent of a French Regiment had volunteered to serve as American Marines.

quarters in Philadelphia in August 1798 but this was only temporary. In June 1800 he transferred the headquarters to the new federal capital of Washington. He established the Marine Corps Barracks, founded the Marine Corps Band and did much to give the new Corps a feeling of *esprit de corps*. In April 1800 he became the Corps' first Commandant.

The War of 1812

The early Marines were involved in numerous naval actions with the French. After the overthrow of the French monarchy, the French displayed open contempt for the United States. They seized US shipping and impressed their seamen. Congress, disgusted with these series of belligerent acts, ordered the US Navy to seize any armed French ships acting in a warlike manner in US waters, and to recapture seized American ships. In the two years or more of this undeclared war the US Navy captured 85 French vessels. Finally February 1801 saw an end to this conflict between two nations which proclaimed

the same democratic ideals. After a prolonged discussion with Napoleon Bonaparte, the arguments were settled. The Marine Corps was drastically reduced by a cost-conscious Congress. The 12 May 1802 witnessed President Thomas Jefferson order the discharge of all Marines except those on board ships and a 17-man detail for each of the five Naval Yards. In the next year Marine strength slipped to 453 enlisted and 23 officers. It would stay at that level for six years.

Between the War of Independence and the War of 1812, the United States was involved in another extended skirmish. The Marines' next adversary was the Barbary Pirates. These cruel and utterly untrustworthy men were the scourge of the Mediterranean. The US did not win the fight with the Barbary Pirates but demonstrated that this young country was willing to fight

to uphold its honor. The US Navy had rescued imprisoned sailors and Marines by paying their ransom. It was not their greatest hour by far, but it provided valuable experience for the fledgling Navy.

The primary reasons for going to war in 1812 were: (1) the Americans wanted to expand and annex new territory and (2) they wanted to stop British harassment of American sailors at sea. Literally thousands of American citizens were seized by the British at sea. The British even went so far as to seize three American seamen from the decks of the US Navy frigate *Chesapeake* by force. When the United States declared war on Great Britain, they were engaged in a major war with Napoleon. The first Marines to see action were those serving on board the *Constitution*. On 19 August 1812 she sighted a sail and gave chase. The

encounter was to improve the reputation of the US Navy. The *Constitution* opened fire on the British frigate *Guerriere*. Exchanging broadside after broadside, American gunnery proved superior and *Guerriere*'s mizzenmast was blown away. Before the action was over, the British frigate's other two masts were shot down and the US Marines had completely outmaneuvered the British sharpshooters in the rigging. When the engagement was broken off, the *Guerriere* was a defenseless wreck. The American frigates continued to win at sea but the British then ordered that American ships were only to be engaged when there was a numerical superiority of two to one. There were other sea fights but the *Constitution* versus *Guerriere* was one of the most important. Later on Marines under Oliver Hazard Perry defeated the British on the Great Lakes. The final crucial battle of war came a year after Perry's victory. Napoleon had been defeated in Europe and the triumphant regular troops of Wellington's Army were shipped to Canada. With these 28,000 crack troops, the British planned to repeat their strategy of the Revolutionary War: march down the Hudson River Valley from Lake Champlain and cut the United States in half. This might very well have succeeded but for the courage of Thomas Macdonough. He did not have any Marines at his disposal but he did have 200 infantrymen serving as acting Marines. These men had the duty to repel all boarders on Macdonough's ships. The 11 September 1814 witnessed the decisive Battle of Lake Champlain. It was an American victory but the casualties on both sides were heavy. The invasion by the flower of the British Army was stopped. Six weeks later peace was signed, but before word was received the Battle of New Orleans was fought. Major General Andrew Jackson commanded the defense of New Orleans against the hated redcoats and he also had a small band of Marines under Lieutenant de Bellevue. The battle was an overwhelming American victory and the Marines' part was recognized by a grateful Congress. Despite the fact that the Battle of New Orleans was fought after the signing of peace, the 1812 War was over.

Left: *The USS* Constitution *engaged in combat with the* Guerriere *on 19 August 1812. This painting was by Thomas Birch.*
Below: *Seamen aboard the* Constitution *cheer at the news of their victory.*

The Indian Wars

The Corps had its early problems, but once Archibald Henderson became Commandant of the Marine Corps in 1820 a new era began for the Corps. Henderson was to become one of the greatest Commandants of the Corps. His life was devoted to the Corps. He wanted a wider role for his men in shaping the destiny of the United States. Henderson formed the Corps into a fighting unit, he gave his men an *esprit de corps* and sense of fellowship that no other service has since been able to imitate.

The next wars in which the Marines were directly involved were the Indian Wars of 1836. Actually the Marines had nothing to say about their involvement, they were all volunteered by Commandant Henderson. He quickly gathered his men and only leaving a skeleton force at the HQs and the Naval Yards proceeded post haste to Columbus, Georgia, where he was to meet with General Winfield Scott. The entire situation was one of injustice and tragedy. Expansion meant more land, only this time it was Indian land and they did not want to give it up. Jackson had slaughtered the might of the Creek nation at the Battle of Horseshoe Bend on 27 March 1814 and killed over 900 warriors. The Creeks then ceded over two-thirds of their territory, totalling 20 million acres by treaty to the white men. Jackson then invaded Florida in April 1818 and so began the First Seminole War. This resulted in the disgusting Treaty of Camp Moultrie in

which the Seminoles agreed to be moved onto a reservation. But there was one individual who was determined that his people were not going to be cheated of their ancient lands. His name was Osceola and he was the warrior chief of the Seminole nation.

The Second Seminole War was about to begin. Osceola launched a surprise attack against a party of soldiers commanded by Major Francis Dade near Fort King and killed every man, except three who managed to escape. His next fight was against General Duncan Clinch and 500 regular troops at a crossing of Withlacoochee River. Again Osceola's men inflicted a grave defeat upon the hated white man. The Navy dispatched Commodore A J Dallas' West India Squadron to Florida to help. The first Marines to land were commanded by 1st Lieutenant Nathaniel Waldron of the *Constellation*. The Marines performed various duties through the campaigns which followed but Henderson was ready to take the offensive by late 1837. His Marines were at the crucial Battle of the Hatchee-Lustee which led the chiefs to ask for a conference in February 1838. It appeared as if the war was finally over. Commandant Henderson was rewarded for his active part in subjugating the Seminoles by promotion to Brigadier General. He was the first Marine officer ever to hold general officer rank. But the war was not yet over, because Osceola managed to enter the encampment and discourage the chiefs from honoring the treaty. The war could have gone on forever but Osceola was captured in October by Brigadier General Jessup who violated the flag of truce which the Indian chief had come under. Osceola was imprisoned at Fort Moultrie, South Carolina and the chief died there from malaria. The Seminole Wars were a caricature of justice, and prejudice against the Indians was rampant; all the government could see was that the Indians were holding up America's future. The United States needed to expand and these lowly Indians were in the way. They were to be brushed aside as if they were scum. By 23 July 1838 the last Marines left Florida and had reported back to Washington.

Between 1840–1847 Marines were involved in the Wilkes Exploring Expedition, and the 33 Marines attached were the first to see Tarawa, Makin and the other numerous islands of the Central Pacific. The Marines were also represented during the annexation of California in 1846. During the Mexican War which followed, Marines saw action at Vera Cruz, Tampico, Tuxpan, Tabasco, Chapultepec and ultimately the heart of Mexico City. The end of an era was at hand; the grand old gentleman of the Corps, Commandant Henderson, died on 6 January 1859 after 36 years as Marine Corps Commandant.

The years preceding the Civil War saw the Corps take part in a number of actions to protect the interests of American businessmen around the world and also save the lives of American citizens: Buenos Aires, 1852; Nicaragua, 1853; Montevideo, 1855; Paraguay, 1855; Fiji Islands, 1855 and 1858; Puget Sound, 1856; the Isthmus of Panama, 1856. The most significant actions were the opening of Japan, 8 July 1853 and the shelling of the forts protecting Canton, China, 1856.

During the Mexican War Marines gained invaluable first-hand experience of combat. They took part in the first amphibious landing in American history at Vera Cruz in March 1847 (right). Below right: *Winfield Scott's entry into Mexico City on 14 September 1847.* Below far right: *The fall of Mexico City.*

Name	Location	Date	Unit
Sergeant Richard Binder	Fort Fisher	1864–65	USS *Ticonderoga*
Sergeant Henry Denig	Mobile Bay	1864	USS *Brooklyn*
Orderly Sergeant Isaac Fry	Fort Fisher	1865	USS *Ticonderoga*
Sergeant Michael Hudson	Mobile Bay	1864	USS *Brooklyn*
Corporal John Mackie	Drewry's Bluff	1862	USS *Galena*
Sergeant James Martin	Mobile Bay	1864	USS *Richmond*
Sergeant Andrew Miller	Mobile Bay	1864	USS *Richmond*
Orderly Sergeant Christopher Nugent	Florida	1863	USS *Fort Henry*
Corporal Miles Ovaitt	Mobile Bay	1864	USS *Brooklyn*
Corporal John Rannahan	Fort Fisher	1865	USS *Minnesota*
Sergeant James Roantree	Mobile Bay	1864	USS *Oneida*
Private John Shivers	Fort Fisher	1865	USS *Minnesota*
Corporal Willard Smith	Mobile Bay	1864	USS *Brooklyn*
Orderly Sergeant David Sprowle	Mobile Bay	1864	USS *Richmond*
Private Henry Thompson	Fort Fisher	1865	USS *Minnesota*
Corporal Andrew Tomlin	Fort Fisher	1865	USS *Wabash*
Sergeant Pinkerton Vaughn	Port Hudson	1863	USS *Mississippi*

Medal of honor winners – Civil War

Total: 17

The Civil War

The Civil War was the Marine Corps' next trial. At the beginning of the conflict, Corps strength was 1800 men; Congress authorized the strength to be increased to 3167. This was the only legislation which allowed the Marines to increase their strength for the entire war, and it would never exceed 3900 men at any time. During the war, in which brother fought brother and on occasion father fought

Above: *A detachment of Marines marches past the Marine Barracks in Washington DC, 14 September 1861.*
Below: *Marines disembark in Tokyo Bay during Perry's expedition to establish trade with Japan.*

son, 148 Marines were killed in battle, 312 died of disease and 131 were wounded. The event which had the most profound effect on the Corps was the creation of a special amphibious battalion in the summer of 1861. This battalion only lasted for approximately six months before being disbanded, but it was a part of the most important undertaking of the entire war, the blockade of the South. This was at first a paperwork exercise because the Union Navy could not adequately seal off 3000 miles of coastline and blockade over 180 separate ports and harbors. The first amphibious operation of the Corps took place when Lieutenant Colonel Reynold's Amphibious battalion was ordered to take Hilton Head Island on the south side of Port Royal Sound, South Carolina. A hurricane hit the small squadron while it was sailing near Cape Hatteras and wrecked a large portion of the support vessels. The amphibious attack was called off, but Flag Officer Samuel DuPont decided to bombard the forts protecting Port Royal. DuPont ran by the two strongholds, Fort Walker and Fort Beauregard, and shelled them both with steady and continuous broadsides as he sailed by. The rebels abandoned both forts, the Marines landed and took possession of them and

set up garrisons. The Stars and Stripes once more flew over South Carolina. On 25 March 1862 the Marines were ordered by DuPont to return to Washington. This spelled the end of a newfangled idea but it was ultimately to change the whole destiny of the Marine Corps. Amphibious landings were an important step forward.

The Marines were confined mainly to ship actions with the Navy during the Civil War. This was because they had no actual function in a fixed land battle as yet. They continued to be useful to the Naval commanders and were used during the assaults up the Mississippi, Mobile Bay, on the *Monitor* and *Merrimack* at Hampton Roads and were directly involved in the capturing of Mason and Slidell aboard the British ship *Trent*. The Marines were used at the discretion of the Navy and eventually took part in the Peninsula Campaigns. When Lee surrendered to Grant at Appomattox Court House, the war was over and the South had the long and arduous task of reconstruction. It would not be an easy job but it had to be done. With the war finally over, the Marines were no longer needed to work the huge naval guns, they were not even trained to land or attack a beach or fort. The question arose: What do we need a Marine Corps for? Amphibious operations were to be the key to the future of the Marine Corps.

The Spanish-American War

In the 30 years which followed the Civil War the Marine Corps managed to survive by the skin of its teeth. Only 2000 men remained in the Corps and there was pressure to abolish it altogether. In November 1876 Brigadier General Jacob Zeilin retired as Commandant. President Ulysses Grant appointed Colonel Charles McCawley as the next Marine Commandant. The way was now open for reform. He immediately improved training techniques for recruits, initiated a new promotion scheme for professional officers and spent a lot of time on actual recruitment. McCawley's new breed of officers were all graduates of the US Naval Academy at Annapolis. They were to dominate the Corps for the next 50 years. A real character in the history of the Marine Corps was appointed as the 14th leader of the Marine Band in 1880, John Philip Sousa. His most famous march *Semper Fidelis* became the official Marine Corps march. McCawley continued to improve the *esprit de corps* and appearance of the Corps until bad

health caused him to retire in January 1891. He died of a heart attack only two months later. His successor was Colonel Charles Heywood.

Heywood was another hard and competent worker who only lived to improve the efficiency and public image of the Corps. He did just that. He fought with gusto against those who were set on disbanding the Corps. He led the Corps through the Spanish-American War and the Philippine Insurrection. He was promoted to Brigadier General in 1899 and Major General in 1902 by a special act of Congress. Upon his death in Washington in 1915, he was buried in Arlington Cemetery with full honors.

The next test for the Marine Corps was the Spanish-American War. Despite the important Pinckney's Treaty of 1795 and the equally important Adams-Onis Treaty of 1819–1821, relations between Spain and the United States had never been cordial. By the 1890s Spain had lost most of its empire, but in the Caribbean it still had Cuba and Puerto Rico. In the Pacific it retained the Philippines and Guam. The war in 1898 was another of Spain's continuing efforts to keep what remained of its empire. It was sparked off by Cuba's efforts to win its freedom and by the growing nationalism and

imperialism that swept the United States. It was also a foretaste of American power in the 20th century. In March 1898 after the unexplained sinking of the USS *Maine* in Havana harbor, war fervor increased in the United States. Spain did not want war with the United States. In fact she even went so far as to offer an armistice but feelings were running high and this was no longer acceptable. From the very beginning Spain was doomed to defeat; it was a most uneven contest.

Commandant Heywood ordered his men to assemble on 16 April 1898. The country was screaming for revenge against the Spanish murders of the *Maine*. The slogan now was: "Remember the *Maine*." Heywood's Marine Battalion of 646 men embarked at Brooklyn, New York on board the USS *Panther*, whose destination was Key West, Florida. The base at Key West was too far from the main theater, so the battalion was transferred to Guantanamo Bay. The Marines spent the majority of the summer there and

Left and right: *Transports and troops prepare for the landings in Cuba in 1898.*
Below: *Marines got a brief taste of action against the Spanish after they landed at Guantanamo Bay in 1898.*

when the US Navy demanded the surrender of Manzanillo they stood ready to go in and take it. The Spanish garrison surrendered on 13 August and in another two weeks the Marines were back home in Portsmouth, New Hampshire. The 1st Marine Battalion was the only Marine Expeditionary Force to serve in the war. While the war was being won in Cuba, Commodore Dewey sailed his understrength Asiatic Squadron into Manila

Bay on 1 May 1898 and destroyed the Spanish Pacific Fleet. On 3 May Dewey's Marines landed on Philippine soil and took the Cavite Naval Station, including its armaments and dockyards. The Spanish then surrendered Corregidor and Manila to Dewey. He became a national hero overnight. His position was extremely dangerous though, as he was low on vital ammunition as well as supplies. He had no army to actually move in and control

On 1 July 1898 General Shafter launched an attack on the small village on El Caney, outside Santiago. The Spanish at Santiago eventually surrendered on 17 July.

Boxer Rebellion

Fighting at Las Guasimas, which was blocking the road to Santiago, in June 1898.

the ground. He notified Washington of the situation and requested that Emilio Aguinaldo, the revolutionary Filipino leader, be sent to Manila. Aguinaldo upon arriving asked Dewey to declare the Philippines independent but the Commodore did not have this sort of authority. In less than two years Aguinaldo would be leading Filipino guerrillas against the US Marines. Reinforcements were on the way to the Philippines. On 20 June the USS *Charleston*, which was escorting troops, stopped at Guam in order to seize it for the United States. The ship fired on the aged Fort Santa Cruz in the harbor at Apra, and two Spanish officers rowed out and gave their apologies for not being able to return the salute. They did not even know that they were at war. Guam was occupied by a Marine force under Lieutenant John Myers. In 1899 a battalion of Marines was dispatched to garrison Guam, and Marines remained on Guam until World War II.

Back in the Caribbean, the Army attacked Santiago and Teddy Roosevelt's Rough Riders charged up San Juan Hill. The Spanish troops were beaten on the ground, and the Spanish fleet attempted to break out of the harbor and escape. This was not to be, the American naval squadron was lying in wait and destroyed the entire fleet except for four ships. Spain was now completely finished as a world power. In July the Army attacked the southern coast of Spanish-held Puerto Rico. The Marines landed under 1st Lieutenant Henry Haines on 27 July and raised the colors on top of the former Spanish customs house. By 12 August hostilities had ceased. The four-month war had transformed the United States into a major world power. The Marines had proved that although they were a small outfit they could deploy rapidly, conduct amphibious operations like that of Guantanamo Bay and could be utilized by the Navy to strengthen and garrison advance bases. The war increased the prestige of the Marines besides giving them practical experience and a foretaste of what was to come in 20 years.

After the Spanish-American War, the people of the Philippines who had been fighting the Spanish believed that the Americans would give them their long-awaited independence. This was not to be the case. The United States had launched her imperial policy and had no intention of granting the Philippines its independence. After all the USA had only just secured its possession. The US Army controlled Manila and Cavite, but the insurgents had control over the rest of Luzon. The Army gradually built up its strength and went into the field against these "rebels," but this left a gap in the defenses, so the Marines were requested to protect Cavite Naval Station and garrison outposts around it. Plans were drawn up to build a new naval base at Subic Bay, and in December 1899 117 Marines moved to Olongapo under the command of Captain H L Draper. By spring Draper's Marines had eliminated the insurgents around Subic Bay. More Marine reinforcements were arriving, and by 1900 the detachments at Cavite and Olongapo manned 12 outposts and 5 lighthouses. But this buildup was stopped abruptly when the Boxer Rebellion endangered the foreign legations at Tientsin and Peking. The Marines in the Philippines were the closest troops available for rapid deployment. Once again they were on their way to a new adventure.

Peking, the Imperial Capital, was a city under siege. The Boxers had effectively cut all communications in and out of the city. A relief expedition was dispatched under British Vice-Admiral Sir Edward Seymour, consisting of 2129 men from eight countries. Seymour utilized the railroad from Tientsin to Peking to move his men as it appeared to be the quickest means of transport. He never considered that the Boxers might tear up the tracks, destroy the stations and pollute the water supplies, which they did. Seymour's expedition found itself trapped halfway between Tientsin and Peking. Seymour ordered his men to fall back to Yangtsun; on 19 June carrying 264 wounded men, he decided to go the rest of the way to Tientsin by boat down the river. On 13 June 1600 Russian troops reinforced the foreign settlements outside the walls of Tientsin. This brought the defending force up to 2400 men. Meanwhile the foreign navies off Taku hit the four forts defending the mouth of Pei Ho River on 17 June. The only navy not to participate in this action was the American squadron under Rear Admiral Kempff, who felt that he did not have the authority to enter such an action. The Taku forts were captured by assault troops and now the foreigners were fighting the Chinese armies which had been staying out of the entire affair. The Tientsin settlement came under intense bombardment and enemy infantry assaults. All Chinese attacks were beaten off but the garrison was now running out of ammunition. A British civilian, James Watts, accompanied by three Cossacks made a heroic ride for help to Taku. A force of 140 US Marines who had only just landed from Cavite departed immediately under Major Tony Waller. Waller's men were joined on the way by 440 Russian infantrymen. This small relief column was stopped by a blown-up bridge and had to fight from village to village until finally casualties became too great to continue. They managed to retreat to their previous camp. The arrival of a British contingent brought the column's strength

to 2000 men and they started out again. The Marines were in the advance guard and this time they fought their way through to the foreign settlements. After resting for only 12 hours, the column marched on to relieve Seymour's battered relief expedition which was trapped eight miles from Tientsin at the German Hsiku Arsenal. By 26 June the relief force reached Seymour and the cheers went up. Now joined together, this force of over 4000 men proceeded to Tientsin.

Back at Peking the foreign legations and settlements were besieged by the irate Boxers. On 20 June the famous 55-day siege of Peking started. The Marines manned the southern section of the Tartar City Wall with their German counterparts. The Marines kept a standing force of 15 men on the 40-foot wide wall. On 27 June the Chinese made their only attempt to assault the wall and were wiped out by intense fire from the defending Marines. The conditions inside the legation compound deteriorated as the siege progressed. Adequate sanitation was

impossible, the stench was unbearable, rations were low, the heat was up to 110 degrees and the torrential rains were driving the trapped staff to the point of insanity. By 3 July 25 percent of all professional military personnel had been either killed or wounded. The Marines continued to drive back attack after attack as the situation in Peking steadily declined. The situation in Tientsin was no better. The ancient walled Chinese city was now garrisoned by 12,000 Imperial troops and 10,000 Boxers. The allies had a force of 14,000 men with which to take the walled city. Colonel Robert Meade, Commander of the 1st Marine Regiment, also had charge of the US Ninth Infantry giving him an effective fighting force of 1021 men. He was under Brigadier General A R Dorward of the British Army. Dorward was in no way a natural leader of men; he did not inspire the confidence of his troops.

Marines were the spearhead of the force which relieved Peking during the Boxer Rebellion in 1900.

A battalion of Marines on parade in the Forbidden City, following the recapture of Peking in August 1900.

Medal of honor winners – Boxer rebellion 1900

Name	Location	Unit
Sergeant John Adams	Tientsin	1st Regiment
Corporal Harry Adirance	Tientsin	1st Regiment
Corporal Edwin Appleton	Tientsin	USFS *Newark*
Private Erwin Boydston	Peking	USS *Oregon*
Private James Burnes	Tientsin	USFS *Newark*
Private Albert Campbell	Tientsin	1st Regiment
Private William Carr	Peking	USFS *Newark*
Private James Cooney	Tientsin	1st Regiment
Corporal John Dahlgren	Peking	USS *Oregon*
Private Daniel Daly	Peking	USFS *Newark*
Private Harry Fisher	Peking	USS *Oregon*
Sergeant Alexander Foley	Tientsin	1st Regiment
Private Charles Francis	Tientsin	1st Regiment
Private Louis Gaiennie	Peking	USFS *Newark*
Private Henry Heisch	Tientsin	USFS *Newark*
Private William Horton	Peking	USS *Oregon*
Private Martin Hunt	Peking	USS *Oregon*
Private Thomas Kates	Tientsin	1st Regiment
Private Clarence Mathias	Tientsin	1st Regiment
Private Albert Moore	Peking	USS *Oregon*
Drummer John Murphy	Peking	USFS *Newark*
Private William Murray	Peking	USFS *Newark*
Private Harry Orndoff	Relief Expedition	USFS *Newark*
Corporal Reuben Phillips	Relief Expedition	USFS *Newark*
Private Herbert Preston	Peking	USS *Oregon*
Private David Scannell	Peking	USS *Oregon*
Private France Silva	Peking	USFS *Newark*
Gunnery Sergeant Peter Stewart	Relief Expedition	USFS *Newark*
Sergeant Clarence Sutton	Tientsin	1st Regiment
Private Oscar Upham	Peking	USS *Oregon*
Sergeant Edward Walker	Peking	USS *Oregon*
Private Frank Young	Peking	USS *Oregon*
Private William Zion	Peking	USS *Oregon*

Total: 33

The attack against the South Gate of the walled city was to result in 700 casualties through this man's incompetence. Throughout the day-long battle the Marines were in the thick of the fighting. By 0300 hours on 14 August 1900 the Japanese destroyed the South Gate and the allies rushed through the gate. Sunrise saw the city in allied hands. After this ferocious fight with the Chinese, the allies built up their forces for the final assault on Peking and the relief of their still besieged legations. The Chinese armies were in a total state of disarray, and with the allies closing in on them at Peking from Tungchow, launched one more concerted attack against the legation. It failed. The allies entered Peking on the morning of 14 August. The siege was over. The Marines remained in Peking until 28 September. They were finally withdrawn on 11 October and sent back to the Philippines. This short but stiff intervention in Chinese affairs had now enmeshed the United States in Asian rivalries which were to last for generations.

The Philippine Insurrection

In June 1900 Major General Arthur MacArthur, Commanding Officer, US Army, Philippines granted an amnesty to all guerrillas in one last attempt to bring an end to the fighting. It was turned down without so much as a second glance. The guerrillas had been hoping that the United States Presidential election would see the Democratic Party win and thus stop annexation. This was not to be; William McKinley was elected and the guerrillas' hopes were dashed to the ground. General MacArthur (the father of Douglas MacArthur) immediately launched a "get tough" program against all insurrectionists. When the 1st Marine Regiment returned to the Philippines from China in October 1900, this was the scene which greeted them. With the return of the Marines from China, the Corps' strength jumped to 1678 men, who were organized into a brigade. It consisted of two regiments, each of two battalions, with an additional battalion utilized with the fleet and two com-

panies of artillery. The 2nd Regiment and Brigade Headquarters went to Cavite. The First Regiment was dispatched to Olongapo, near Subic Bay. They were now ready for their primary missions of providing security for the naval stations and to administer the local military government. Both regiments carried out these duties with gusto and a sense of duty which far surpassed their army counterparts. By 1901 Aguinaldo had been captured and reluctantly swore an oath of allegiance to the United States. For all practical purposes this ended the Philippine Insurrection. On 4 July 1901 Judge William Howard Taft became the first Civilian Governor of the Philippine Islands.

Although organized resistance was at an end on Luzon, some of the outlying islands still had a few hard heads who failed to give in. It was these which the Marines came up against during the following year. At 0645 hours on 28 September 1901 450 Filipinos armed with bolos assaulted the US 9th Infantry's C Company which was garrisoning Balangiga, on the southern end of the island of Samar. The garrison had just risen and were in the middle of eating their breakfast. The surprise attack was a

complete success. Army casualties were 48 killed in action; only 28 men survived the attack and 13 of these were wounded. The insurrectionists made away with all the rifles and over 28,000 rounds of ammunition. This was not going to be taken lightly; a Marine Battalion, commanded by Major Tony Waller and 314 men, was dispatched immediately to Samar to exact reprisals against the Filipinos. Waller's battalion came under the operational command of Brigadier Jacob "Hell-roaring Jake" Smith, who maintained his headquarters across the strait at Tacloban, Leyte. Smith ordered Waller and his second in command Captain David Porter to strike against the enemy with all possible speed. The Marines made daily combat patrols and succeeded in recovering some of the captured weaponry which had belonged to C Company. But the enemy kept fading back to the safety of the jungle. Finally, the steady persistence of the Marines paid dividends, the enemy concentrated its entire force upriver from Basey at the volcanic formations of the Sohoton cliffs which rose to a vertical height of over 200 feet from the river. There they dug in just like the Japanese in World War II. This did not deter Waller; he ordered

Captain Porter and Captain Hiram Bearss, with two columns, to attack and destroy all villages and houses in the surrounding area. Having completed their assignments, both columns met on the left bank of the river directly below the formidable cliffs. The date was 16 November 1901. The Marines were now ready to go in and finish their ghost-like prey. The order to advance was given but upon reaching the crest of the cliff, it was discovered that the enemy had once again escaped undetected. The Marines thought they were robbed again but a scout returned and stated that the enemy was on the other side of the river. Porter ordered his men to move quietly and opened fire on the enemy encampment across the river. The result of the intense fire which the Marines brought to bear was 30 of the enemy killed. Porter's column then threw caution to the wind and without support crossed the river and scaled the cliffs on the other side of the river. The Filipinos fired a few rounds and then ran away as fast as they could go. Waller wrote commendations for both Porter and Bearss, as well as two NCOs, Gunnery Sergeant John Quick and Corporal Harry Glenn.

The most terrible disaster to hit the Marines was yet to come. Ironically enough, it was not inflicted by the insurrectionists but the jungle. The US Army had determined that maps would be required to string telegraph wire between the garrisons in southern Samar: from Basey across the island to Lanang on the east coast, and from Basey west coast to Balangiga on the southern coast. Waller decided to make the attempt himself with only 50 Marines. When the actual crossing started it was composed of Waller, Porter and Bearss, 1st Lieutenant Alexander S Williams, 2nd Lieutenant Frank Halford, 50 Marines, 33 native bearers, 2nd Lieutenant C De Lyles and a couple of soldiers from the Seventh Infantry. It was not a large force to cross a jungle never before entered by white men.

The first portion of the trip only took four days. This was from Basey to Balangiga. Waller took a column of men along the coast; while Bearss commanded a column on a parallel course two miles inland. Waller and his men went around Lanang by boat, and by 28 December were moving up the Lanang River. He decided to cross the island and make for Basey. On 29 December stiff rapids forced them to abandon the boats and continue on land. The soldiers then parted company with the main force and returned with the boats to Lanang. The Marines were beset by obstacles along the entire journey. The first one was the jungle-covered mountains. In some places it

was so thick that at 1200 hours the sun was completely blocked out. The place was crawling with snakes and reptiles which made the going that much tougher, for the men had to be extremely careful of the venomous reptiles. They crossed and recrossed the meandering Lanang, and although forced marching sometimes up to 12 miles, the real distance covered however was only about four or five miles. The going was difficult to say the least; for anyone who has never seen the Philippine jungles it is hard to describe it adequately. The Marines had to crawl over huge logs, move through thick underbrush, put up with severe and unexpected tropical rain storms, fight the damp and extreme mountain cold, and finally swamp fever which did not distinguish between ranks but laid everyone low. Rations were cut in half as they could find nothing to supplement them in the jungle. The Marines were almost exhausted when the trail completely disappeared and the Lanang River changed its direction and started flowing east. It was the last straw. The entire outfit came to a halt.

Waller knew what would happen if his tired men did not move on, so he selected 14 of the strongest Marines and pressed forward. He hoped to meet with Captain Robert Dunlap who after establishing a base camp was to have been en route to meet Waller's column. On reaching Dunlap Waller planned to send help to the men he had left behind. Porter and Bearss remained with the rest of the scouting party and were to follow Waller as best they could. Waller's advance force found a jungle clearing with bananas and managed to recoup some of their lost strength. Waller then sent a message back to Porter telling him to build rafts to float back down the Lanang River as the advance party could make no further progress. Porter's force stopped and proceeded to attempt to build enough rafts to accommodate the entire expedition. The only problem was that no suitable wood for the rafts was available. Rafts could be made but they would not float with the weight of the men. The Marines were stymied again. Bearss wanted to advise Waller of this personally. With only two men, Corporal Murphy and a Filipino scout, he set out to find Waller. Bearss made contact with Waller at the clearing and Waller decided once again to advance and left a message for Porter attached to a pole stuck in the middle of the trail. This was to prove fatal; communications between the two parties would never again be established. Porter meanwhile had not heard from Bearss or Waller and was getting worried about what to do next, as his men were feverish and down to their last ration of

food. With Gunnery Sergeant Quick, six Marines, six Filipinos and himself, Porter started on the long march back to Lanang. Lieutenant Williams was left in charge of the remaining Marines. Unknown to Porter, Waller and Bearss were moving westward through practically impassable terrain. After managing to cross several rivers, they came to a quite substantial river where they met five Filipinos. These natives were quite surprised to see white men come out of the tropical rain forest and looked at them in bewilderment. Waller explained to them that he needed a guide to Basey. After obtaining a guide and a short rest, Waller's party started out once again for Basey, totally in the hands of their native guides. On 5 January 1902 they crossed two more rivers, and then remarkably discovered Captain Dunlap on his way to establish the supply depot. All of Waller's men were put into a cutter and got to Basey on 6 January. Without even a rest for himself, Waller returned to search for Porter's group for a further nine days before being stricken by fever himself and being forced to return.

The luckless Porter was still trying to make his way to Lanang. Only this time it was even worse for the men as they had no food whatsoever and were utterly exhausted. They made it back to where they had left the boats on the forward journey and had to leave another four men behind as they were unable to travel. Their feet were torn and bleeding, leeches hung off their bodies and fever had left them practically senseless. On 11 January Porter finally reached Lanang. An Army relief party was dispatched to rescue the four men left behind immediately. Although Waller, Bearss and Porter had an extremely gruelling time, the ones who had the worse of it were Williams and his 61 men. He realized that if they stayed behind they would all starve to death. So he ordered his men back down the trail in the path of Porter. These pitiful survivors, hardly able to crawl, were left on the trail to die one by one as they fell, unable to keep up. The weather was absolutely no help, and it rained for 18 days without a break. The trails were turned into a muddy and impassable quagmire. The Filipinos were in better shape than the Marines and managed to find some nourishment to sustain them. Three of the Filipinos even attempted to kill Williams with his own pistol but could not make it work. Another tried to kill him with a bolo but the Marines managed to protect him by beating off the attacks with sticks. The Army relief expedition finally reached them on 17 January. Of the surviving Marines, 18 had to be stretchered out and nine were presumed dead in the jungle. Waller's fateful expedition into the heart of Samar was over but one more chapter was still to be written.

Waller was lying ill at Basey with fever when Gunnery Sergeant Quick arrived on 20 January with a message from Porter. Ten days prior to Quick's arrival Waller had ordered the execution of a Filipino for spying. Porter recommended that Waller order the immediate execution of all the natives who had threatened mutiny on the return march with Lieutenant Williams. Waller asked Quick, the hero of Guantanamo Bay, what his personal opinion was, Quick replied, "I would shoot them all down like mad dogs." Dunlap and Day were also asked for their opinions and they both concurred with the execution recommendation. A firing squad was organized and 11 Filipinos were executed. Waller reported his actions in writing to Brigadier General Smith and stated his reasons for carrying out the executions. After recovering from his fever, Waller returned to Cavite on 29 February, where he learned that Major General Adna Chaffee had levelled charges of murder against him for killing 11 Filipinos. Waller could not believe his ears and the newspapers at home went so far as to call him "The Butcher of Samar." It was an election year and as usual politics played an extremely important part in the conduct of the

Medal of honor winners – Philippine insurrection 1899–1902			
Name	*Location*	*Date*	*Unit*
Captain Hiram Bearss	Samar	1901	1st Regiment
Private Howard Buckley	Luzon	1899	USS *Helena*
Sergeant Bruno Forsterer	Samoa	1899	USS *Philadelphia*
Sergeant Harry Harvey	Benictican	1900	1st Regiment
Private Henry Hurlbert	Samoa	1899	USS *Philadelphia*
Private Joseph Leonard	Luzon	1899	USS *Helena*
Sergeant Michael McNally	Samoa	1899	USS *Philadelphia*
Captain David Porter	Samar	1901	Marine Barracks, Cavite
Corporal Thomas Prendergast	Luzon	1899	USS *Helena*
Total: 9			

investigation. Secretary of War, Elihu Root and General Nelson Miles, Chief of Staff, ordered an immediate court-martial. A military court was convened on 17 March 1902 to try both Waller and Day for violations of the 58th Article of War. It was apparent that the powers to be were out to hang Waller. On the court-martial board were seven Army officers and six Marine officers. Leaving aside the election year politics, there was an internal power struggle going on within the ranks of the Marine officers on the board as well. Waller's name had been mentioned as a possible successor to Commandant Heywood when he retired and the officers on the board were prepared to do anything to better their own chances of securing this coveted post. The trial went on for 18 days. On the last day, Waller stated that after careful consideration from all points, "I ordered the 11 men shot. I honestly thought I was right then, I

believe now that I was right." The court acquitted Waller by 11 to two. Major General Chaffee totally disapproved of the acquittal but had no choice but to abide by the verdict. Lieutenant Day was also tried and acquitted for his part in the affair. Finally Brigadier General Smith was also tried and found guilty but President Theodore Roosevelt retired him early. The entire affair damaged Waller's career in the Corps, and although nominated for the Commandant's position on two subsequent occasions, he never held that most coveted of all Marine posts. Thus ended another chapter in the annals of the Marine Corps.

United States Marines patrol the tropical jungles near Olongapo, Luzon in the Philippines during the mopping up operations against guerrillas in 1900.

This mobile artillery unit based at Marine Base, Quantico, Virginia was ready to fight in any country in the world in 1917.

From the Halls of Montezuma

The Marine Corps and American Imperialism

For the next three decades, US Marines would serve in the Caribbean as an essential tool of American foreign policy. The so-called "Banana Wars" saw this US foreign policy implemented and enforced by the Marines. President Theodore Roosevelt's 1904 corollary to the Monroe Doctrine, whereby he stated the United States' unilateral right to intervene in the Western Hemisphere was the authority to do so. During these first 30 years of the 20th century, Americans built railroads and promoted industrial activity; various companies like United Fruit Company established plants and became the forerunners of the present day multinational corporations, ushering in the era of international big business; other companies with mining interests moved in; and with land so cheap big plantations thrived. The poor countries of this area could not adjust to their new situation. Revolutions and military coups were a thing of the future; a direct result of the local governments becoming dominated by corrupt officials, a single crop agriculture system and the suppression of crucial social reforms. The only ones to actually suffer were the indigenous population. This period witnessed the United States Marines land in Panama, Cuba and Mexico; and they made a further three interventions: Nicaragua in 1912–1913 and 1926–1933; Haiti in 1915–1934; and finally the Dominican Republic in 1916–1924. The Marines ensured that foreign powers would not enter into the private American sphere of influence in the Western Hemisphere. They also guaranteed law and order. These interventions resulted in the United States becoming "hated Yankee Imperialist Pigs" by the end of the 1930s. The scene was now ready for the next American power play.

The Panama Canal

The first step which took the Marines into the Caribbean was the need for a canal across the Isthmus of Panama, which was then a vital part of Colombia. In 1901 US Marines landed in the isthmus to protect American interests in the area and at the request of the Colombian government which would not run trains across the isthmus without American protection. Later the Colombian government would regret this action but could not go back on it. American business interests caused Colombia to lose the isthmus and the valuable revenues which the canal would have brought into its coffers. The Marines provided security for the railroad by riding as train guards. Meanwhile the Colombian troops and Panamanian rebels engaged in skirmishes throughout the countryside, neither side able to get the upper hand. Behind the scenes, Washington was aiding and abetting the rebels and New York businessmen were financing the Panamanians in their fight against their masters. Little did the Panamanian rebels then realize they would only be exchanging one hated master for another: the Colombians for the Americans, who would later seize the canal as their just due.

On 22 September 1902 Lieutenant Colonel Benjamin Russell landed at Colon on the Caribbean side with a Marine battalion of 342 men. He assigned one company to remain in Colon and then proceeded with the remainder of his force to Panama City on the Pacific side. These Marines also served as train guards until they reembarked on 17 November. On the international front the government of Colombia refused to ratify the treaty which would grant the canal building concession to the Americans. On 2 November 1903 the cruiser *Nashville* arrived at Colon and the Panamanians declared an open revolt against Colombia. The very next day 4000 Colombian troops arrived at Colon. The captain of the *Nashville*, Commander John Hubbard, refused to allow them to use the trains to quell the

Below: *Marines undergo intensive training at a Rifle Range in Winthrop, Maryland in October 1913.*

revolution in Panama City. A blatant interference in the internal affairs of another nation's sovereign rights, which could undoubtedly have been handled with more finesse. Hubbard sent ashore a landing party and finally managed to encourage the Colombian commander to reembark his men. The Republic of Panama was officially declared, and a Marine battalion arrived in the transport *Dixie* on 5 November. Major John Lejeune (a future Marine Corps Commandant) landed two companies at Colon and relieved the landing force from *Nashville*. The Marines only stayed for 24 hours but that was sufficient time for the revolution to succeed. The United States as usual recognized the new republic and procured the rights to the isthmus canal. The final days of 1903 saw the Navy dispatch an expeditionary force to Yaviza and Réal de Santa Maria, the two major points from which the Colombians could launch a punitive attack into Panama. By December the sailors were reinforced by a company of Marines commanded by Captain Smedley Butler. They were in turn reinforced by a Marine detachment from the *Boston*. Lejeune had established a base camp ashore and was joined by an additional battalion of Marines commanded by Major Louis Lucas. Finally on 3 January 1903 Brigadier General Elliot, the Marine Corps Commandant, personally arrived with a further Marine contingent of 635 men and assumed overall command of all Marine forces in Panama. This was the first occasion that a Commandant had personally taken to the field since Henderson in the Seminole Wars. Elliot organized the Marines into a provisional brigade, composed of two regiments, commanded by Lieutenant Colonels Waller and Biddle. The Marines spent the majority of their time mapping the country and making notes of the defenses of the city and the canal. By the middle of February 1903 Colombia had given assurances that she would not invade Panama. The need for the brigade in Panama had receded and therefore it was gradually withdrawn to Guantanamo. At the end of March the only remaining Marines were Lejeune's 1st Battalion, 1st Marines. In the fall of 1904 the Panamanian army attempted to take control of the government. The Marines got ready for action against the rebels. The Panamanian commander, seeing that the Marines meant business, disbanded his army. Finally in 1911 the United States Army assumed the defense of the Panama Canal Zone. The Canal opened in 1914 and the Marines take the credit for ensuring that it would remain American. The

next step in the Caribbean was to Cuba.

Although the Marines undertook three landings in Cuba, they did not actually fight there. The Marines spent most of their time providing security for American mining and sugar interests. The first landing occurred on 13 September 1906, when Major Albertus Catlin disembarked with 130 Marines from the cruiser *Denver* at Havana and camped in front of the Presidential palace. They only stayed ashore until the next morning when they were ordered back to their ship by the US State Department. The Marines were back in Cuba on 28 September when the 2800 man Provisional Marine Brigade landed at Havana. This time the Marines, commanded by Colonel Waller, stayed longer and did not depart until 22 January 1909. The third and final landing occurred on 28 May 1912 when another revolt broke out. The Marines landed at Guantanamo Bay and were utilized to protect American property. The Marines made other insignificant landings in Cuba for various reasons after 1912 but none of which amounted to anything.

The next Marine intervention was in Mexico and it was caused by an insult to the American flag. The date was 1914 and Mexico was being torn apart by internal power struggles. In this tense climate, the USS *Dolphin* sent a whaleboat ashore on 6 April 1914 to load supplies at the dock of Tampico. The revolutionary leader General Victoriano Huerta was in the process of taking Tampico. Some of his more energetic men captured seven US sailors and the paymaster and threw them into a Mexican jail. They were only held for less than an hour but Rear Admiral Henry Mayo interpreted this as an affront to the American flag. He demanded an immediate 21-gun salute from Huerta to the American flag in the way of an apology. Huerta refused and President Wilson asked Congress to approve the utilization of armed force to win the respect due to the flag. He received the sanction of Congress and had already dispatched a fleet of seven battleships to intercept supplies which Huerta had anxiously been waiting for. These supplies were being transported on the German ship *Ypiranga*. Although wanting to seize the arms and ammunition aboard this vessel, the United States had to be extremely careful not to become involved in an international incident with Germany. Therefore this seizure had to be accomplished after the supplies had been delivered. The 1st Marine Advanced Base Brigade was already in Mexican waters and was just waiting for the word to go in. The Brigade was

commanded by Colonel Lejeune. On 21 April Marines landed and took the Customs House at Vera Cruz. The Marines on the next day made a house-to-house search to secure the city from a determined sniper attack from the rooftops. In the afternoon Lieutenant Colonel Charles Long's 1st Regiment landed; and Colonel Lejeune assumed command of all Marines ashore and they were organized into the 1st Marine Brigade. The Marines were still securing the city on the second day. The third day witnessed the Marines complete the search for snipers and the center of Vera Cruz was occupied. By the end of the fourth day over 7000 troops were ashore. On 29 April Colonel Waller took over command of the Marine force as the senior officer on the scene. The *Ypiranga* stayed at Vera Cruz for several weeks but did not unload its cargo. It finally sailed and managed to unload its cargo at another Mexican port. On 15 July General Huerta left Mexico on board the *Ypiranga* and the revolution was a failure. The United States never received an apology to the flag but Huerta had been deposed.

Nicaragua

The first major intervention in the Caribbean began in 1912 in Nicaragua. The Conservative president Adolfo Diaz, faced with strong Liberal opposition in local internal affairs, told the Americans that he could no longer guarantee their protection. He requested that the United States intervene to protect its citizens and interests in Nicaragua. Thus began the first phase of the Marine intervention in Nicaragua. The Conservatives accepted complete American domination of their economic program, as the US were keeping them in power. On 14 August 1914 the first contingent of Marines landed. Major Butler was their commander and his force totalled 354 men. This advance force of Marines immediately moved to the capital of Managua. More reinforcements were starting to arrive at Corinto on the Pacific coast, and Butler dispatched a force of ten Marines and 40 sailors by train to make contact with them. This turned out to be an embarrassment, as the rebels stopped the train and forced the American personnel to walk back to Managua on foot. The Marines did not take very kindly to this insult. Butler was furious and rounded up 190 Marines, then moved to Corinto in an attempt to open up the railroad. He made contact with the rebels on two separate occasions and turned the tables on them both

Below: *1st Sergeant Major John Quick and Captain Monk Delano hoist the Stars and Stripes over the Hotel Terminal in Vera Cruz, Mexico on 21 April 1914.*

times. He reached Corinto without further incident and after holding a conference with the US naval officers there returned to the capital. More Marines were on the way: Colonel Pendleton arrived on 4 September with the 1st and 2nd Battalions, 1st Provisional Regiment, totalling 753 Marines. He assigned one battalion to Corinto and with the other moved to Managua. Pendleton after assessing the situation in the capital assigned Butler the task of clearing the railroad from Managua through Masaya to Granada. Butler assembled his force armed with machine guns and 3-inch field artillery and moved out. He ran straight into the middle of a fully fledged battle between the Liberal Army commanded by General Benjamin Zeledon and the government forces near the town of Masaya. He immediately set up a meeting between Zeledon and Rear Admiral William Southerland, and after much bickering was allowed to pass unhindered through the Liberal lines. Apparently word of this agreement did not reach all the rebels because snipers opened up on the train at Masaya. Some of the Marines deployed to return the fire, but when Butler ordered the train to race out of the troubled area, he left behind some of his men. Captain Nelson Vulte commandeered a hand-car and assembled the majority of the Marines and sped after Butler's train. Butler halted the train a few miles away and Vulte joined up with him and let him know that there were still some Marines behind in rebel hands. Butler was ready to start a war himself to get his men back when he received an abject note of apology from Zeledon together with his three lost Marines. Upon reaching the outskirts of Granada, Butler encountered the rebel army of General Luis Mena. Butler, never one to mince his words, ordered Mena to surrender or he would destroy his forces. Mena surrendered at the very last minute. Meanwhile back at Managua, Pendleton heard a rumor that Butler was cut off and besieged in Granada. Pendleton immediately raised a relief column and advanced against Granada, bringing with him as many supplies as he could possibly manage for the starving inhabitants of the city. The only remaining force which still offered any sort of resistance to the government troops was Zeledon's army which controlled the 500-foot Coyotepe hill dominating the railroad and the town of Masaya. On 2 October the Marines, a force of US sailors and the government army prepared to assault the hill. The hill was bombarded with heavy artillery fire throughout the 3rd to soften up the rebels. At 0515 hours on 4 October the

Americans assaulted the hill. The actual battle lasted for only 40 minutes and resulted in Zeledon being killed by his own troops when he attempted to escape from the town. American casualties were extremely light considering what could have happened if the enemy had really fought back; seven Marines and sailors were killed during the action. After the fall of Masaya, Leon surrendered to Lieutenant Colonel Charles Long, and the revolution was over. By January 1913 the majority of Marines were withdrawn from Nicaragua, but a force of 105 men were left at US legation in Managua as a sort of stopgap. Once again the United States had stepped in and interfered in the internal affairs of another country. This type of intervention was going to become a habit which the United States would find hard to break. The people of Managua resented the American interference in their internal politics and vented all their spleen against the Marine contingent in Managua. The problem which the Americans faced was that they acted in support of an unpopular government and once elections were held the Liberals would be in power with an overwhelming majority. In 1924 the first fair and impartial election was conducted and a coalition government of sorts was inaugurated. On 4 August 1925 the remaining Marines were withdrawn from Nicaragua. By the end of October the country was once again in turmoil. Finally, with no other choice left to him, President Calvin Coolidge was forced to send the Marines back to Nicaragua to protect the lives and property of American citizens. On 6 January 1927 the Marines once again landed at Corinto and marched to Managua to protect foreign nationals in the capital. At Bluefields the 2nd Battalion, 5th Marines, established a neutral zone. The 51st Company was left to garrison the newly established neutral zone and the rest sailed through the Panama Canal for Corinto. By 7 March Brigadier General Logan Feland had arrived and took command of the 2000 Marines in Nicaragua. The Marines were in Nicaragua for their second fully fledged intervention.

President Coolidge sent his personal envoy to Nicaragua to negotiate a settlement. This was in the person of Henry Stimson. A truce was arranged but only until the elections of 1928. A further force of Marines arrived, bringing the total to 3300 men, and they were organized into the 2nd Marine Brigade. The Marines fought in Nicaragua for the next five years; they established a *Guardia Nacionale de Nicaragua*, who were trained and officered by Marines. The jungle

fighting in Nicaragua gave the future leaders of the Marine Corps much needed experience; for instance, Carlson, Edson, Puller, Rowell and Schilt all served in Nicaragua. These men were to be the core of the Marine Corps in the 1940s. On 2 January 1933 the second Nicaraguan Intervention ended with the last Marine pulling out. The way was now open for the next military intervention. The Marines had learned much and gained expertise in jungle fighting and the Haitian intervention capitalized on this experience.

Haiti

One of the most severely criticized interventions in the Caribbean was in Haiti; it was the longest and definitely the most ineffective. It began at 1750 hours on 28 July 1915 when two companies of US Marines landed at the navy yard at Bizoton, near the Haitian capital of Port-au-Prince. The Marines could not have picked a worse time to land. On 27 July 162 political prisoners in the National Penitentiary were liquidated on the orders of the President, Vilbrun Gjuillaume Sam. This brutal and senseless killing so angered the people that they stormed the French Legation and literally hacked Sam to pieces. While that was going on, another crowd entered the Dominican Legation and killed the warden of the prison. It was to this welcome that Captain George Van Orden and his Marines landed. They marched on the capital and sustained fire from the rebels, resulting in some minor casualties. Upon arriving in the capital, guards were placed immediately at various foreign legations. Sam had brought an interlude of peace to Haiti's short but very violent history. It only lasted four months before another revolution broke out led by Rosalvo Bobo, who had the support of the "cacos." President Wilson had strong feelings about Haiti mainly because the Germans were showing a great interest in exploiting Haiti's weakness. With all of Europe at war, Germany could utilize a vital foothold in Haiti. Rear Admiral William Caperton took command of Cap Haitien, the second largest city and the main port, on 1 July. Caperton immediately ordered the Marines from Guantanamo to move up and by the next day they were landing. Minor clashes occurred during this period resulting in two sailors being killed. On 31 July five companies of the 2nd Marine Regiment, commanded by Colonel Eli Cole, left Philadelphia *en route* for Haiti. They landed at Cap Haitien and the tension which had been so intense started to ease. At Port-au-Prince Caperton took the Fort Nationale and subsequently ordered all Haitian soldiers to leave the city. Resistance was brutally dealt with.

The struggle between Rosalvo Bobo and Sudre Dartiguenave intensified. The latter was the presiding officer of the Haitian Senate who was prepared to accept complete US domination. Bobo attempted to stop the American-bribed Haitian Senate from electing Dartiguenave as President but was foiled when Marines arrived to protect the legislature while they voted. Of course Dartiguenave was elected as President – that was a foregone conclusion. However the price was very steep, a ten-year treaty with the United States that placed Haiti's customs under complete US control and made it mandatory that the Haitian constabulary be officered and

Left: *An early Lewis gun, operated here with an improvised sling. This light machine gun was used by the Marines until 1917.*
Below: *Marines on patrol outside Vera Cruz following the brief intervention in July 1914.*

Above: *Early Marine aviators during a break in a training session in Miami. The US air arm was rapidly expanded after 1913.*

commanded by Americans. The treaty furthermore could be renewed for an additional ten years by either side. It attempted to give the invasion a semblance of legitimacy. The United States had no legal right to interfere in the internal affairs of another nation; however it was to do this time and time again. By the end of August the Marines were organized into the 1st Marine Brigade and totalled over 2000 men. Colonel Waller was the commander of all US forces in Haiti.

The cacos in the north once again showed that they were not yet to be written off. They fought with the Marines at the port town of Gonaives and managed to place the garrison in a state of siege. Major Smedley Butler and 1st Lieutenant Alexander Vandegrift (later to earn fame at Guadalcanal) decided to make for Gonaives with all possible speed. Butler personally led the 7th Company against the cacos and drove them from the town. Butler initiated an immediate program to find and destroy all cacos no matter where they were. Consequently the greater part of northern Haiti was burned to the ground by fanatical Marines obeying orders. At Cap Haitien Colonel Cole commanded the 1st Battalion, 1st Marines, when the cacos began to cut off the food supply to the city. Cole tried to reason with the cacos at first, and then sent a five-company punitive Marine force out to destroy them. The cacos surrounded this force and when two other companies succeeded in reinforcing the first group they were all surrounded. Cole decided then and there to teach the cacos a lesson, he brought a detachment of sailors ashore from the *Connecticut* and led the entire battalion out to do battle with these rebels. After a long gruelling fight the Marines finally won and drove the cacos back but one thing was learned by the Marines, the cacos were no pushover. Waller advanced north with the 11th Company and landed at Fort Liberté, marched to Ouanaminthe near the border with the Dominican Republic. He then established Marine garrisons along the border. Marines continued to reinforce the northern areas in which the cacos had the upper hand. Cole and Butler transferred their headquarters inland to Grande Rivière du Nord and dispatched even stronger patrols into the countryside. On 24 October Butler commanded a deep reconnaissance patrol into the Haitian mountains. They advanced as far as a deep ravine near the small outpost of Fort Dipite. The cacos were watching their prog-

ress and picked this ideal location to ambush the mounted Marine unit from three sides. The Marines managed to fight their way clear and make for a semi-defensible position about one mile away. They were harassed the entire way but succeeded in keeping the cacos at bay. Gunnery Sergeant "Fighting Dan" Daly, the holder of the Medal of Honor from the Boxer Rebellion, returned to the ravine that night alone to recover the patrol's only machine gun which had been lost during the initial fighting. All through the night, the cacos kept up light sporadic fire on the Marine positions but did not manage to inflict any casualties. At daybreak Captain William Upshur and 1st Lieutenant Edward Ostermann took two detachments, and Daly commanded a third, which drove the cacos away. Fort Dipite was taken next. Daly, Upshur and Ostermann all received the Medal of Honor for their heroic efforts during the fight. It should be noted and with great pride that this was Daly's second Medal of Honor. The Marines now spent all of their efforts in chasing the elusive cacos; the rebels would fight here and there, but usually ran to fight at a place of their own choosing. But this running had to stop eventually, the cacos were trapped finally at the old French Fort called Rivière. Fort Rivière was on the very top of a

Below: *1st Lieutenant Alfred Cunningham was the first Marine officer to be designated a naval aviator.*

mountain, just south of Grande Rivière du Nord.

On 17 November a force of Marines and sailors during a night move surrounded the fort. At 0730 hours on 18 November Butler blew his whistle and the Battle of Fort Rivière had begun. The cacos were taken totally by surprise for a change. They attempted to escape by jumping over the walls and into the brush but the Marines were waiting and just machine gunned them as they ran for cover. The only entrance to the fort was through a small one-man tunnel in the exterior wall. Major Butler and Captain Low, the latter commanding the 15th Company of Marines, ran through heavy rebel fire and made the wall. The Marines were now against the wall and waiting for the first man to go through into the fort proper. Sergeant Ross Iams got tired of waiting and stated, "Oh, hell, I'm going through," he made it through and was quickly followed by Private Samuel Gross, Butler's orderly. Butler himself was the third man through the gap. Hand-to-hand fighting occurred for the next 20 minutes, resulting in over 50 cacos being killed. Butler had the fort blown up so that it could not be utilized again by rebel forces. Sergeant Iams, Private Gross and Butler received the Medal of Honor for their part in the destruction of Fort Rivière. Butler became only the

second Marine, along with "Fighting Dan" Daly, to ever receive two Medals of Honor for two separate engagements. Butler had received his first only the year before at Vera Cruz. Waller was ordered to limit their activities as tremendous political interest was being awakened in Washington against the Marines. A group of Senators publicly condemned them for the barbaric actions in Haiti. In the preceding two years hostilities virtually ceased until 5 January 1916 when a large number of cacos attacked the Marine Provost Marshal's building in Port-au-Prince. The small Marine garrison on duty succeeded in driving the rabble away utilizing only billet sticks. Caperton issued a proclamation on 1 February which stated that all military and police functions would be assumed by the Gendarmerie d'Haiti. The first initial phase of the Haitian intervention was now for all practical purposes finished. The Marine Brigade was then gradually reduced in size until only 600 men were left in Haiti. The Marine occupation of Haiti left two marks upon the people of Haiti: a vigorous and total hate of the American pigs and distrust of American imperialism. The Gendarmerie d'Haiti was trained totally by the Marines under Butler, who had been promoted to Major General. The Gendarmerie were able to handle the majority of situations which they were confronted with. But sporadic fighting continued throughout the next few years, it was interrupted by a brief redeployment caused by United States entry into World War I. Finally the Gendarmerie could no longer handle the fighting which broke throughout all of Haiti once again. The Marine Brigade now commanded by Brigadier General Albertus Catlin was reinforced from Guantanamo; and the 4th Marine Air Squadron (MAS), VO-9M, came in with the first 13 planes. The leader of the cacos was a much respected Haitian by the name of Charlemagne Peralte whose hatred of the Marines and Gendarmerie, and all who would oppress his people would survive until his death. This man was a natural leader, who would test the Marines to their utmost limits. Sporadic fighting continued between Peralte's cacos and the Gendarmerie.

Marine Sergeant Herman Hanneken, who also held a commission in the Gendarmerie had established a small intelligence service within his organization manned by local Haitians. He arranged for three of his men to defect to the caco camp, thus giving him inside information on the movement of Peralte and his army. Hanneken made several diversionary attacks against Fort Capois and even arranged for it to look as if he was wounded in one of the skirmishes. He dispatched a portion of his garrison to Cap Haitien and spread the rumor that he feared a caco attack on Grande Rivière du Nord because of his understrength forces. Jean Conze, one of Hanneken's spies urged Peralte to attack the city. Peralte sent over 1000 cacos against Grande Rivière du Nord. The attack was set to be launched on the night of 31 October. Peralte would await the news of the battle at Mazare only a short journey away. Meanwhile Marines commanded by Major James Meade secretly reinforced the garrison the night before the expected attack. Hanneken and Corporal William Button and 20 men went to Mazare with the intention of capturing or killing Peralte whichever opportunity presented itself. Hanneken's small force managed to sneak past the caco pickets and seeing Peralte talking with a woman near a camp fire opened up.

Hanneken personally shot Peralte in the chest twice with his .45, while Button kept the cacos pinned down with his BAR. Hanneken's men dug in that night and the next morning slung Peralte's body over the back of a mule and returned to Grande Rivière du Nord. Upon returning Hanneken learned that Meade's garrison had driven off the caco attack and inflicted heavy casualties on them. The very next day as if not sated by the killing so far, the Marines moved against Fort Capois and the cacos there. After intense fighting Fort Capois fell to the Marines. Hanneken and Button were

Right: *This 3-inch field piece was used by the Marines during the intervention in the Dominican Republic, 1916.*
Below: *The United States Marines prepare for a Decoration Day Parade in Shanghai, in 1913.*

awarded the Medal of Honor for their extraordinary gallantry in action, but Button did not live to appreciate this honor since he died of malaria at Cap Haitien. Hanneken was to go still further and ultimately receive a commission, and retire as a Brigadier General. Peralte's second in command, Benoit Batraville, became the new leader of the cacos, but did not last very long although he did manage to raise an army of over 2000 men. He was caught by a Marine reprisal patrol led by 2nd Lieutenant Edgar Kirkpatrick, and shot dead by Sergeant William Passmore. With the death of Batraville the caco movement ended. World War I also ended and the argument the Americans had used, that they were worried about German intervention in the Caribbean no longer held water. With outcries from home the Marines started to withdraw but a contingent of Marines still remained. The 1920s were years of relative peace and quiet but the Marines in Haiti could sense the resentment of the people at every turn. They were hated as "Yankee Imperialistic Pigs" and there was nothing they could do to change that opinion. If anything it hardened as the years went by, each generation making the next vividly aware of the outrages inflicted upon them by the hated Yankees. The Marine Brigade was finally withdrawn from Haiti on 15 August 1934. Thus ended 19 years of continuous occupation by a foreign power.

The Dominican Republic

The final intervention in the Caribbean was initiated in the spring of 1916. The rest of the world was not interested in this little skirmish. Europe was bogged down in the trenches and millions of men were dying every week in the front lines. President Woodrow Wilson, an ex-college professor, was worried about the security of the Caribbean and especially its stability. The government of the Dominican Republic had resigned and walked out, leaving the entire island in turmoil. This was not the first time that the Dominican Republic, previously known as Santo Domingo, was torn asunder by political strife. The country had gone through 70 years of fighting of one sort or another, the victor never staying in power for very long. But the man responsible for establishing the precedence for American imperialism and constant interference in the Caribbean was President Theodore Roosevelt, of Rough Rider fame, during the

Spanish-American War. In 1904 the Dominican Republic was totally bankrupt and could not even pay the smallest of its debts. Consequently President Roosevelt put extreme pressure to bear upon the country's government to allow the United States of America to collect their custom duties and pay off their debts. This high-handed action established the precedent which became the model for America's imperialist ways in Latin America and the Caribbean. For two months in 1911 over 750 Marines, 2nd Provisional Regiment, waited in naval transports off the shore of the island while the politicians and diplomats attempted to set up some sort of arrangement for at least temporary peace.

The scene was now set for the next act. On 5 May 1916 150 Marines, from the 6th and 9th Companies, commanded by Captain Frederic Wise were transferred from Haiti to provide security for the US and Haitian legations. Various political factions were battling throughout the capital city of Santo Domingo, and the entire city was in a state of unrest and tension. It was like a powder keg with a lit fuse, just waiting to blow up. On 6 May the president resigned and the tension increased. A battalion of Marines and one of naval personnel occupied the city on 15 May. The people offered no resistance but they were extremely angry at yet another foreign intervention into their internal affairs. The Marine garrison in the city kept increasing until finally Colonel Theodore Kane assumed command after arriving with a further three companies of Marines. The end of May saw no noticeable change in the atmosphere but Marine strength was now at a peak of 750 men. The time was now ripe for the Marines to go into action against the rebels who were controlling the north coast at Puerto Plata. Major Charles Hatch commanded a Marine and naval detachment which landed in the face of heavy enemy fire on 1 June with the intent of driving the rebels out of their positions. But it was the heavy naval bombardment which actually drove the rebels from their positions, and also enabled the Marines to capture one of the two forts guarding the city. The rebels retreated south in the hope that the Marines would not pursue them and that they would have a chance to regroup. The pressure was far from removed and in fact increased. Captain Wise landed on 26 May in the early morning and captured Monte Cristi. The 4th Marine Regiment, commanded by Colonel Joseph Pendleton, arrived too late for this fray, but Pendleton took command of all Marine

forces on the island. The 4th Marines landed at Monte Cristi and advanced up the Zaza River. It was Pendleton's intention to march 75 miles up the river valley to Santiago where the rebels had established a temporary headquarters. On 26 June Pendleton led his picked 837 men unit against Santiago. Simultaneously the 4th and 9th Companies left Puerto Plata to rendezvous with Pendleton inland at Navarette. Both units then were to launch a coordinated attack against the rebels' positions at Santiago. This clearly shows to what lengths the United States government was willing to go in its effort to suppress all anti-American sentiment in the Dominican Republic. Could this be true of the country which preached "liberty, equality and justice for all"? Yes, because that is exactly what it did, and would do again in its effort to protect what it considered to be its sphere of influence.

Colonel Pendleton advanced over 24 miles through tough terrain and on the second day of the march arrived at the two fortified ridges of the Las Trench-eras. These ridges were believed to be impregnable. A very strong rebel force occupied two lines directly across the Marines' line of advance. The next move was left to the Marines, and the rebel commander had no doubt but that the Marines would retreat in the face of his superior positioning. He did not reckon on the mettle of the United States Marines. At 0800 hours under the cover of an artillery barrage and protected on the flanks by machine

guns, the regiment did what the rebel commander least expected – attacked. The regiment was stopped dead in their tracks by superior enemy fire. However the two battalions were not acting in synchronization as planned; to rectify this Major Robert Dunlap, the regimental Chief of Staff, assumed command of the advance elements personally. Dunlap led the next charge and drove the enemy from their front-line positions. The Marines brought their superior rifle fire to bear against the second line of trenches and the enemy was beaten. The battle took less than one hour and resulted in one Marine killed in action and four wounded. This action is worthy of note because it was the first time that the Marine Corps had attacked an enemy position with artillery and machine-gun support – another precedent had been established. Immediately afterwards Pendleton ordered the advance to continue, but the Marines got bogged down in the mud-filled roads and the terrain became worse and progress slower. Pendleton progressed only ten miles that day before stopping to make camp for the night. Even on that night the weary Marines could not have a proper rest; the enemy launched

Right: *Captain Roy Geiger, a future Marine general in World War II, joined the Naval Aeronautic Station at Pensacola in 1916.*
Below: *Men of the 4th Marines protect their headquarters in Santiago, Dominican Republic, in July 1916.*

a night attack on the camp but was driven off without inflicting any casualties. On 3 July at Guayacanas, the road was blocked by another rebel force which was entrenched but undaunted, and the Marines charged straight through and drove them out. Casualties were one killed in action and ten wounded. Two Marines were awarded the Medal of Honor for their heroic part in this action: 1st Sergeant Roswell Winans, who cleared a jammed gun while exposed to continuous enemy fire; and Corporal Joseph Glowin, who continued firing his Colt gun after being severely wounded and under heavy enemy fire. Meanwhile Captain Julian Smith commanding the 6th Company fought off an enemy attack against the Marine supply train. On 4 July, Independence Day, Pendleton's tired Marines entered Navarette.

The other two companies which were to rendezvous with Colonel Pendleton at Navarette had a brief skirmish with the rebels and were delayed. This resulted in Lieutenant Colonel Hiram Bearss, the winner of the Medal of Honor at the Sohoton Cliffs in Samar, taking the Marine detachment from the *New Jersey* to reform them and also assuming command. The Bearss outfit then advanced until they came to the rebel-held Alta Mira ridge where the railroad ran into a tunnel. Bearss had to eliminate the enemy from their position guarding the railroad. He personally led 60 Marines through the tunnel to cut off the enemy's escape route. The rebels seeing what was about to happen abandoned their positions and fled into the mountains. One Marine Corps' story states that Bearss stood on top of a trench, bullets whizzing by him and shouted at a private who just happened to stick his head up for a look around: "Get down, you damn fool! You'll get shot." Bearss' outfit linked up with Pendleton at Navarette on 4 July and the next stage of the campaign was about to unfold. The next day witnessed a delegation from Santiago come out and meet with Pendleton in an attempt to stop further bloodshed. The Marines peacefully entered Santiago the next afternoon without a shot being fired. They rounded up the remnants of the rebel force as well as their leaders. The first round was now finished. By the fall of 1916 there were 1785 Marines serving in the Dominican Republic – quite a force. The Marines were reorganized into the 2nd Marine Brigade.

All was not a bed of roses between the Marines and the people of the Dominican Republic, especially those from near the capital. The temporary president wanted to have national elections by late November 1916 but the US State Department opposed this on the grounds that the rebel leader Desiderio Arias would be elected with an overwhelming majority and he was definitely not suitable for American interests. Friction increased between the Marines and the people, which eventually resulted in a military government being imposed on the Dominican Republic. President Wilson approved this move on the recommendations of the State Department. This was to be the most radical step that the United States would take into the internal affairs of any Caribbean nation. It was not made for the benefit of the people of the Dominican Republic but in the best interests of the United States. The military governor was Captain Harry Knapp. He imposed rigid censorship and forbade the carrying of firearms, which was as traditional to the Dominicans as gun-toting was in the Old West. The Dominican Civil government in a very strong protest all resigned and refused to serve in the military government. Knapp was forced to appoint all Americans to key government positions and this did not meet with any form of approval from the Dominicans. Pendleton was placed in charge of the Departments of the Interior, Navy, Police and War; and Colonel Rufus Lane, another Marine, was placed in charge of the Departments of Foreign Relations, Public Administration and Justice.

Meanwhile in the north, the Dominican Governor Juan Perez refused pointblank to submit to the American occupiers. Perez believed the Americans to be invaders. The Dominicans held some prisoners at Fortaleza and fearing that they would be released after learning about the establishment of a military government, 1st Lieutenant Ernest Williams acted on his own initiative and seized the fort. He took 12 Marines with him and rushed the main gates of the fort. Eight of his 12 men were brought down by enemy fire before reaching the gates. Williams saw that the gates were being closed and threw himself against them forcing an opening. He was immediately confronted by a Dominican soldier who was going to fire a rifle at him practically pointblank when his sidearm jammed. Seeing death in front of him, he witnessed Drummer Schovan attack the soldier and deflect the rifle. Williams and his remaining four Marines then took possession of the fort. Lieutenant Williams received the Medal of Honor for his courageous act.

The main force of the military government in the Dominican Republic was the 2nd Marine Brigade commanded by Brigadier General Pendleton. The primary task of the Marine Brigade was to disarm the populace and pacify the countryside. The methods which the Marines utilized left much to be desired, and instead of neutralizing opposition to their occupation only succeeded in strengthening it. Hundreds of patrols

Medal of honor winners – Caribbean

Name	Location	Date	Unit
Major Randolph Berkeley	Vera Cruz	1914	2nd Advance Base Regiment
Major Smedley Butler	Vera Cruz	1914	2nd Advance Base Regiment
Major Albertus Catlin	Vera Cruz	1914	3rd Regiment
Captain Jesse Dyer	Vera Cruz	1914	2nd Advance Base Regiment
Captain Eli Fryer	Vera Cruz	1914	2nd Advance Base Regiment
Captain Walter Hill	Vera Cruz	1914	2nd Advance Base Regiment
Captain John Hughes	Vera Cruz	1914	2nd Advance Base Regiment
Lieutenant Colonel Wendell Neville	Vera Cruz	1914	2nd Regiment
Major George Reid	Vera Cruz	1914	3rd Regiment

Haitian campaign 1915

Major Smedley Butler	Fort Rivière	1915	CO detachments
Gunnery Sergeant Daniel Daly	Fort Dipite	1915	2nd Regiment
Private Samuel Gross	Fort Rivière	1915	USS *Connecticut*
Sergeant Ross Iams	Fort Rivière	1915	USS *Connecticut*
1st Lieutenant Edward Ostermann	Fort Dipite	1915	1st Brigade
Captain William Upshur	Fort Dipite	1915	2nd Regiment

Dominican Republic 1916

Corporal Joseph Glowin	Guayacanas	1916	Artillery Battalion
1st Lieutenant Ernest Williams	San Francisco de Marcoris	1916	4th Regiment
1st Sergeant Roswell Winans	Guayacanas	1916	4th Regiment
Total: 18			

Above: *Applicants arrive at the Recruiting Depot, Parris Island in South Carolina, 1917.*
Right: *Marines man 3-inch guns on board the USS* Pennsylvania.

and punitive expeditions were dispatched throughout 1917. But the most important accomplishment of the year was the surrender of the main rebel leader Vincentico Evangelista to Colonel George Thorpe. Right after Evangelista had surrendered, he was murdered while attempting to escape from custody. The rebels believed that their main and most respected leader was eliminated because of his anti-American beliefs. With Evangelista's death all organized resistance to American policies stopped. The Marines remained in the Dominican Republic until September 1924 when they were withdrawn. The only important outcome of the occupation of the Dominican Republic was that it left a heritage of intense hatred of Americans throughout the Caribbean.

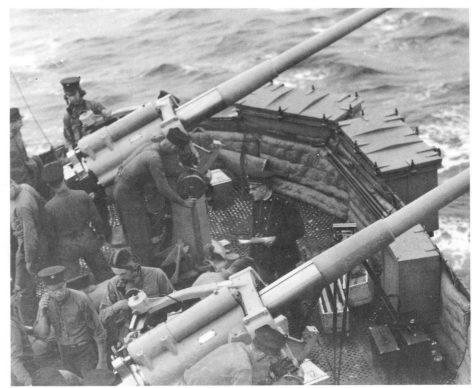

Two men in a shell crater during heavy fighting in the Meuse-Argonne area of France in 1918.

Into a New Age

World War I

The summer of 1914 saw the flames of war spread like wildfire through Europe. The Germans invaded Belgium, then outflanked the French defensive fortifications and headed straight for Paris. It looked as if the war might be of a very short duration. As usual the military estimates were wrong again – far from being a short war, this conflict went on for four years and cost millions of lives. The French managed to halt the German drive on Paris at the ferocious Battle of the Marne. The front lines then settled down into a long and intermittent trench war.

The United States tried to retain its neutrality and stay out of this European conflict. The international scene had changed so much by 6 April 1917 that President Woodrow Wilson had no choice but to ask Congress for a declaration of war. The Marine Corps only had 13,214 enlisted men and 511 officers assigned at the start of the war. Since the war was not to be one of major naval confrontations, the task of the Marines would be, in the words of Colonel John Lejeune, "the Advance Guard of the Army." The first Marines to be deployed to France as part of General John Pershing's American Expeditionary Force (AEF) were the 5th and 6th Marine Regiments. By 23 October 1917 these two regiments were joined by the 6th Marine Machine-Gun Battalion and formed into the 4th Brigade of Marines, commanded by Brigadier General Charles Doyen. The Marines were now ready for commitment to the front, after years of gruelling training and preparation.

It was 1700 hours on 6 June 1918, the long lines of helmeted Marines were ready, their bayonets were fixed and destiny awaited them. Major Benjamin Berry, Commander 3rd Battalion 5th Marines was leading his men against the German positions in Belleau Wood. The Marines had hoped to have the element of surprise on their side. The Germans, however, were waiting for them with Maxim machine guns and mowed down the Marine files. The first waves of gallant Marines never really had a chance. On the right Major Berton Sibley's 3rd Battalion 6th Marines moved into the battle and were cut down by the concentrated

machine-gun fire. The Marines continued to advance although sustaining heavy casualties so that by nightfall they had a foothold in Belleau Wood. Of the Marine Brigade committed on 6 June, 1087 men were casualties.

The Marines dug in and on 7 June, the Germans shelled them all day and well into the evening. At midnight the Germans counterattacked in an attempt to drive the Marines back. They stopped dead in their tracks. The whole battle was turning into a stalemate. Through 8, 9 and 10 June the Marines tried to advance slowly into the woods but the Germans continued to fight extremely hard for every inch of ground yielded. By 11 June Brigadier General Harbord sent word that the northern part of Belleau Wood belonged to the 5th Marines.

Above: *The US victory at Belleau Wood, for which the Marines took all the credit, was the origin of bad feeling between the Marines and the US Army.*
Below: *Fighting during the Marines' last action in the Meuse-Argonne campaign during World War I.*

TELL THAT TO THE MARINES!

AT 24 EAST 23rd STREET

This recruiting poster for the Marines played on anti-German sentiment. Allied propaganda built up a totally distorted image of the Germans.

That was not the whole truth of the matter, the 5th Marines were far from controlling the northern sector of the woods. The Germans thought the Americans were a bunch of reckless idiots. They nicknamed the Marines *Teufelhunde* – Devil Dogs. The Marines took great pride in this compliment from their enemy. Meanwhile, because of Harbord's premature message to staff, General Pershing, Commander in Chief of the American Expeditionary Force, announced that Belleau Wood had fallen.

This placed the local commanders in quite a predicament. On 12 June they decided it was time to make the news release a fact rather than a fiction. Finally the Marines were starting to push the German lines back and were actually gaining ground in the northern sector of the wood. The Marines again took heavy casualties in the advance but a high percentage was from the mustard gas attacks. The advance continued through 15 June and the Marines gained additional ground in the western sector of the wood. Later that night the Marine Brigade was relieved by the 7th Infantry and the French. In two weeks of running battle the Brigade had lost more than 50 percent of their men in casualties. The Marines were sent to the rear for a much deserved rest while the 7th Infantry attempted to dislodge the Germans from their positions. The 3rd Battalion 5th Marines was brought back in an attempt to clean out the German resistance as the 7th Infantry were not making any ground. Shearer's battalion sustained over 130 casualties on 23 June and was halted. The Marine Brigade was sent forward again. Shearer's battalion was still in the center of the wood. With the entire Brigade moving through the wood the Germans found it very difficult to hold their ground and started retreating. By 0700 hours on 26 June Captain Robert Yowell's 16th Company, 3rd Battalion, was at the northern edge of Belleau Wood. The battalion commander immediately dispatched a message to Harbord: "Woods now US Marine Corps entirely." Thus another chapter was added to the Marine Corps' history. The French were so overjoyed with this American victory that their parliament declared 4 July a national holiday in honor of the victorious Americans. The Army did not like the Marines getting credit for the victories or all the publicity. This was the beginning of a long feud which would be carried over into World War II. It was one of the reasons why US Marines did not fight on the European continent again.

The Germans did not let Belleau Wood set them back. On 15 July 49 German divisions struck toward Paris, crossed the Marne River and seized a bridgehead four miles deep. In the next 48 hours the Germans were thrown back across the Marne and sustained fantastic casualties in the retreat. The tide was turning but the war was not yet over. General Foch decided to strike an immediate counterattack against the German-held Maubeuge highway between Soissons and Château-Thierry. The Marine Brigade was once again called up to the front, and was to move with the 2nd Division. Harbord was now a major general and commanded the entire division. He was a part of the Tenth French Army, and the Aisne-Marne Offensive was just beginning and would not be concluded until the Germans surrendered. The Marines advanced under intense enemy fire, it was some of the most concentrated fire of the war. By 19 July the Germans had succeeded in halting the Marines only one mile short of their objective. In these two days the Brigade had lost over 2015 men killed and wounded. The attack had driven the Germans back from the Marne to the Vesle River, and it had set off the general retreat of the German Army. On 26 July Brigadier General John Lejeune assumed command of the Brigade, and only a couple of days later he was promoted to major general and took over the 2nd Division. Brigadier General Neville resumed command of the Brigade for the duration of the war.

Foch's next move was to eliminate once and for all the St Mihiel salient, the last in the Western Front. The Germans realized that intensive action was going to break out in the St Mihiel salient and at 0100 hours, 12 September started retreating. A few minutes after they started moving back, the bombardment began. The 3rd Infantry Brigade led the attack, the 5th Marines were in support of the 9th Infantry on the right and the 6th Marines supported the 23rd Infantry on the left. There was hardly any

Interwar

resistance to speak of, and by the end of the second day the Marine Brigade took the advance line. Casualties were light; the Brigade sustained 132 men killed and 574 wounded. That night the St Mihiel salient was eliminated.

Meanwhile Foch had already started shifting troops for his next offensive against the Argonne. On 26 September Foch began his great offensive to crush the main German defensive system from the Meuse to the North Sea. The US First Army could not break through the enemy's defenses. It was not until the 2nd Division took Blanc Mont Ridge, on 5 October that the Germans started to retreat. The stage

As air power became more important so more resources were diverted for air defense. Here Marines man an early anti-aircraft gun.

was now set for the Marines' last battle before the armistice was signed. This was the Battle of the Meuse-Argonne and was already in progress. The 2nd Division was placed in the center of Major General Charles Summerall's First Army with the V Corps as its spearhead. On 1 November 1918 the largest field army that the United States had ever mustered was thrown into battle. The Marines fought gallantly as always, through shelled landscape, ruined towns, barbed wire and German defensive positions. The Germans started retreating slowly at first, but suddenly their front collapsed. The Allies still kept up the pressure until the armistice. In the last battle over one million American troops were engaged, and the casualties totalled 117,000 Americans and over 100,000 Germans. The war was ended.

The years between World War I and World War II were extremely hard years for the Marine Corps. The two main problems that the Corps' leaders had to deal with were civilian disgust with anything concerned with the military and the Great Depression. In July 1919 an economy-minded Congress cut the Marine strength to 28,493 men, but the Corps could never even enlist that number. Strength continued to fall through the 1920s and 1930s, so that by 1933, only 15,000 men were authorized. The man who saved the Corps during this trying period was its new Commandant, John Lejeune, a man of political acumen. He fought for his men on Capitol Hill. His greatest accomplishment was the laying of a firm foundation for future Marine amphibious operations because he believed that the future of the Corps was in this direction.

Through the years of hectic peace between the world wars the Marines were kept on their toes by interventions in Vladivostok, 1919; Dominican Republic, 1924; Honduras, in 1924 and 1925; Nicaragua between 1927 and 1933; and Haiti in 1934. During the prewar period, the Marines were very active on the Chinese mainland, serving at Shanghai, Tientsin and Peking. The famous "Horse Marines" serving at the legation in Peking were renowned for their expertise in cavalry drills. By September 1931 Japan was starting her policy of aggression, she had already seized Korea back in 1910 and now she invaded Manchuria. No one was willing at that time to step in and take on this resource-hungry nation. Japan continued to capitalize on the Western world's apparent unwillingness to become involved in the Asian continent again. Things got progressively worse, until finally on 7 July 1937 the Second Sino-Japanese War broke out. During the forthcoming campaigns and fighting, American hospitals, churches and educational institutions across the entire breadth of China were shelled and destroyed by the fanatical Japanese troops. They even went so far as to sink the USS *Panay*, an American gunboat patrolling the Yangtse River. President Roosevelt urged a quarantine against the aggressors but this came to nothing. By early 1941 it appeared imminent that the United States and Japan would go to war. Admiral Thomas Hart, Asiatic Fleet Commander requested that 4th Marine Regiment serving in China be pulled out. On 10 November 1941 orders were received from Washington to evacuate

the 4th Marines, ending the era of the China Marines. However, war was just around the corner, and who could have foretold what the fate of the 4th Marines would eventually be – Bataan and Corregidor were on the horizon.

US Policy in the Far East

The attack on Pearl Harbor was the product of long-term trends in relations between the United States and Japan. For almost 50 years, ever since Commodore Matthew Perry visited Japan in 1853–1854, the two countries although totally different in basic ideology managed to maintain cordial relations. In fact some Americans looked upon Japan as a protégé of the United States in Asia. Japan's rapid industrial growth and relatively simple victory over the Chinese in 1894–1895 were both viewed as nothing out of the ordinary. The turning point in American relations with Japan was the Russo-Japanese War of 1904–1905. From 1905 until the end of World War II, US and Japanese interests often clashed in East Asia and the Western Pacific. World War I saw the Japanese expand their interests in China much to the dismay of the Americans. President Woodrow Wilson unsuccessfully attempted to block Japanese demands at the Versailles Peace Conference. Relations did improve somewhat during the 1920s but steadily declined through the Great Depression years. These various patterns ultimately led to outbreak of hostilities in 1941.

External and internal considerations prompted Japan to expand in Asia and the Pacific area. Japan was determined to guard its national security against all external threats. This was the very reason why the Japanese feared Chiang Kai-shek and his Kuomintang, as it provided leadership, power and direction to Chinese nationalism. This would be a direct threat against Japanese special interests in East Asia, an area where they believed themselves to be dominant. Also Russian and Japanese interests were in conflict over northeast Asia, but that all changed with the complete Japanese victory during the Russo-Japanese War of 1904–1905. The Russian Revolution in 1917 and the ensuing civil war which tore Russia apart prevented her from actively challenging Japan. But the aftermath presented another even more serious problem for the Japanese. Lenin and Stalin coming to power with

Right: *Men of the 2nd Marines parade through the streets of New York on 8 August 1919.*
Below: *Prime Minister Winston Churchill reviews the 6th Marines Regiment on the occasion of his visit to Iceland in August 1941.*

the Communist Party, and their steady industrial development and rapid military expansion was a portent of danger to Japanese interests and future security. By 1939 the Axis was victorious throughout Europe, and England, France, the Netherlands and the Soviet Union were all too weak and preoccupied to block any of Japan's expansion plans. The only two powers left that stood in the immediate way of Japan's manifest destiny were China and the United States of America. The former could largely be discounted, which left the United States as the major outside threat to Japan.

The Sino-Japanese War broke out in 1937 and did not end until Japan surrendered in 1945. After a minor incident at the Marco Polo Bridge near Peking on 7 July 1937, Japan dispatched troops into China, claiming the incident was just provocation. The Chinese under the leadership of General Chiang Kai-shek fought back but were always fighting on the defensive. The United States State Department sympathized with China and thought Japan the aggressor. Roosevelt and Hull took steps to aid China and check Japan. The President initiated a cash and carry policy with Japan and an arms embargo, both of which hurt Japan. Throughout the late 1930s and 1940 the United States contininued to put more and more pressure on Japan in the way of trade restrictions. The Japanese looked on these and the US semi-open aid to China as tantamount to an act of war. On 25 July 1941 the Japanese army seized French Indo-China. Roosevelt reacted immediately by freezing all Japanese assets in the United States. The British and Dutch followed suit and froze Japanese assets in their countries. Without money to buy the oil to drive its ships and armies, Japan had only one option, to take over areas which had their own oil supplies.

Above: *An aerial view of Pearl Harbor months before the Japanese attack.*

Japanese prestige and pride were now at stake. All of these political and diplomatic actions against Japan were the basis for the ultimate decision of the Japanese high command to attack the US Pacific Fleet at Pearl Harbor. The Japanese felt that they were being pushed into acting but they were sure of one thing – the United States would not want to fight a protracted conflict. The Japanese believed that Americans were pampered and lazy, but as Admiral Isoroku Yamamoto stated, the United States could not be defeated in a long war. The Japanese hoped that after a crushing victory over the US fleet at Pearl Harbor they would be able to dictate a fast peace, but this was not to be the case. The scene was now set for the Marines to engage in open conflict with the Empire of Japan – the date was 7 December 1941.

Pearl Harbor

It was another peaceful and uneventful Sunday morning at Ewa Field, Hawaii. This Marine airfield was only four miles from Pearl Harbor. The officer of the day was Marine Captain Leonard Ashwell. He had spent an uneventful night and was looking forward to a nice quiet day. That Sunday morning was 7 December 1941. Ashwell had just left the mess hall when he observed two sections of Japanese bombers flying eastward and another section of Zero fighters coming in at the field. He ran for the guard house to give the alarm. It did little good because after repeated strafing of the Marine field, all 47 aircraft of MAG-21 were destroyed. Two minutes later the Japanese were hitting Pearl Harbor. Colonel Harry Pickett ordered all of his 485 Marines out of the Marine Barracks at the Navy Yard. They set up machine-gun positions and handed out ammunition and weapons. These Marines succeeded in shooting down three enemy dive bombers.

The Japanese surprise attack against Pearl Harbor accomplished exactly what it had set out to do – destroy the American Pacific Fleet and USAAF strength on the ground. Of particular note, when the USS *Arizona* went down, it took with it 108 Marines and a further 49 were wounded. By the end of December 1941, however, the Marines were reorganized and shipped out to reinforce the tiny garrisons at Johnston Island, Midway and Palmyra.

The Marines engaged the Japanese on the ground in only four locations after the Pearl Harbor disaster in China, Guam, Wake and the Philippines. The first two ended practically before they had started. Wake and the Philippines both saw a tough fight.

In China the news was brought to 2nd Lieutenant Richard Huizenga who was directing the loading of supplies and equipment aboard the *President Harrison* at Chinwangtao docks, just northeast of Tientsin. Huizenga ran back to his 21 Marines at the railhead and discovered that they were already surrounded by Japanese troops. A few Marines under Chief Marine Gunner Wilson Lee had managed to break out machine guns and BARs and were going to make a fight of it. Huizenga was allowed by the Japanese to get in

Above: *President Roosevelt, surrounded by his Cabinet, reviews the US fleet on 31 May 1934.*

touch with Major Luther Brown at Tientsin, who gave the order not to resist. In Peking and Tientsin, the Japanese surrounded the Marine Barracks and ordered them to surrender. Colonel William Ashurst, the senior Marine officer at the US Embassy got in touch with Admiral Hart, Commander of the Asiatic Fleet at Manila and requested instructions. Ashurst

Below: *The smoking hulks of the USS* Nevada *and USS* Shaw *in Battleship Row on the Day of Infamy.*

A column of spray rises as the USS West Virginia is hit by a torpedo during the first wave of Japanese bombers. She is on the far side of Ford Island in Battleship Row. On the other side of the island (left) are the USS Detroit, Raleigh, Utah and Tangier. The photograph was taken at 0800 hours on 7 December 1941 as Japanese aircraft were flying over the Navy Yard.

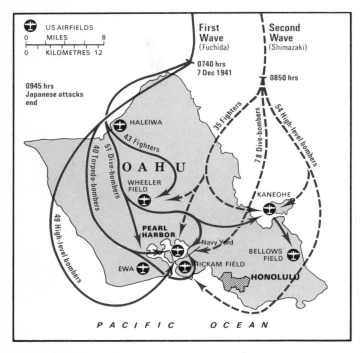

Map labels (left map):
US AIRFIELDS
MILES 0 — 8
KILOMETRES 0 — 12
0945 hrs Japanese attacks end
First Wave (Fuchida)
Second Wave (Shimazaki)
0740 hrs 7 Dec 1941
0850 hrs
35 Fighters
54 High-level bombers
78 Dive-bombers
43 Fighters
HALEIWA
40 Torpedo-bombers
51 Dive-bombers
O A H U
WHEELER FIELD
KANEOHE
PEARL HARBOR
Navy Yard
BELLOWS FIELD
49 High-level bombers
EWA
HICKAM FIELD
HONOLULU
PACIFIC OCEAN

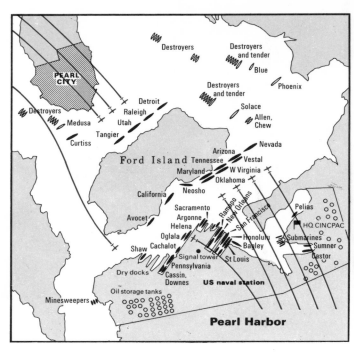

Map labels (right map):
PEARL CITY
Destroyers
Destroyers and tender
Blue
Phoenix
Destroyers and tender
Destroyers
Detroit
Raleigh
Solace
Medusa
Utah
Allen, Chew
Tangier
Curtiss
Nevada
Arizona
Ford Island
Tennessee
Vestal
Maryland
W Virginia
Oklahoma
California
Neosho
Sacramento
Ramapo
New Orleans
Pelias
Avocet
Argonne
San Francisco
Helena
Honolulu
Bagley
HQ CINCPAC
Submarines
Oglala
Sumner
Shaw
Cachalot
St Louis
Castor
Signal tower
Pennsylvania
Dry docks
Cassin, Downes
US naval station
Oil storage tanks
Minesweepers
Pearl Harbor

and Brown then ordered their 200 men to lay down their arms and not to resist. It had been hoped that because they were Embassy guards that they would be repatriated with the diplomatic personnel. This was not the Japanese intention, the Marines were all imprisoned in Shanghai.

On Guam the Marines were no more prepared to resist than their counterparts in China. The Guam garrison was made up of only 153 Marines. At 0827 hours on 8 December Japanese bombers from Saipan hit the island, and there was not adequate defense. Lieutenant Colonel William McNulty was the Marine Commander. The heaviest weapon the Marines had available were .30 caliber machine guns. The Japanese landed 5500 men at Tumon Bay and a further 400 men at Dungcas Beach, at 0400 hours on 10 December. The island governor, Captain George McMillan, ordered the Marines to surrender because he realized just how futile resistance would be.

Above left: *Another aerial picture of Battleship Row under attack, shortly before the final dive-bombing wave. The battleships are (l-r)* Nevada, Arizona *and* Vestal, Tennessee *and* West Virginia, Maryland *and* Oklahoma. *At this point only the* Maryland *and the* Tennessee *had escaped damage.*
Left: *The magazine of the USS* Shaw *explodes. She was berthed near the oil storage tanks which were also hit.*
Right: *The USS* Pennsylvania, Cassin *and* Downes *were all sitting targets for the Japanese dive bombers. The* Pennsylvania *was not hit by the torpedo bombers and the damage inflicted by the dive bombers was quickly brought under control.*

Wake Island

Wake Island is an atoll 3705 km (2302 miles) west of Hawaii, in the Central Pacific Ocean. It consists of three low-altitude islets: Wake, Wilkes and Peale – 6.5 sq km in all, lying in a horseshoe shape on the reef. In 1941 the United States Navy initiated the construction of an air and submarine base which was only half finished at the time of Pearl Harbor. The commander of the atoll was Commander W S Cunningham; the Marine contingent of 447 men was under Major James P S Devereux, and there were 1100 civilians working on various construction projects. The Japanese attacked Wake Island initially on 8 December 1941 at 1200 hours with 36 bombers, just a few hours after the Pearl Harbor strike. But the main fight was still to come; at 0500 hours on 11 December a Japanese naval task force, consisting of cruisers, destroyers and troop transports, struck at Wake Island. Major Devereux, a shrewd strategist, told his men manning the gun batteries to hold their fire and wait until the Japanese ships were well within their range. At 0615 hours the light cruiser *Yubari*, a brand-new ship, and three destroyers sailed to within 4500 yards of the atoll and well within the range of 5-inch gun batteries. The Marines opened up immediately on the Japanese ships. Battery A commanded by 1st Lieutenant Clarence Barninger scored hits on the *Yubari* three times. The light cruiser, unused to this type of coastal batteries, got out of range as fast as it could move. Battery L commanded by 2nd Lieutenant John McAlister on Wilkes Island destroyed the Japanese

destroyer *Hayate*. The *Hayate* was the first enemy surface vessel sunk by US naval forces in the war. The fast shooting Marine gunners then turned their attention upon another light cruiser and succeeded in driving her away also. Battery B, commanded by 1st Lieutenant Woodrow Kessler on Peale Island, also managed to hit a destroyer and cause severe damage. The accurate, in fact superlative, marksmanship of the Marine gunners succeeded in driving off the Japanese invasion force even if only temporarily. Meanwhile, not to be outdone by the coastal gunners, four Marine Grumman F4F Wildcats commanded by Major Paul Putnam took off and attacked the retreating task force. After dropping their initial payload, they rushed back to Wake and rearmed and went back to the attack. The end result of this aerial attack was the sinking of the destroyer *Kisaragi* by Captain Henry Elrod, and further damage to two other destroyers and one transport. This was a total success for the Marine garrison on Wake and when news of their courageous stand reached the States, the cry was "Don't let Wake Island fall."

The Japanese high command was determined to take Wake Island at all costs; it was a matter of pride now, and they could not afford to allow such a small band of men to stand in their way. The American naval commanders attempted to muster a relief force for Wake. This fast carrier force was built around the carriers *Enterprise*, *Lexington* and *Saratoga*. But once again indecisiveness and failure to act rapidly doomed the Marines. Japanese bombers hit the atoll daily, causing damage to the installations and pitiful few aircraft which were so vital to the

Above: *Admiral Chester W Nimitz was appointed Commander in Chief of the Pacific Fleet following the debacle at Pearl Harbor. He was the architect of the Midway victory.*

Above: *Douglas SDB Dauntlesses warm up ready for take off from the USS
Yorktown at Coral Sea. Dauntlesses were used both for reconnaissance and for
dive bombing.*
Below: *The USS Lexington blazes during the Battle of Coral Sea. She suffered
such extensive damage from dive bombers that she had to be scuttled.*

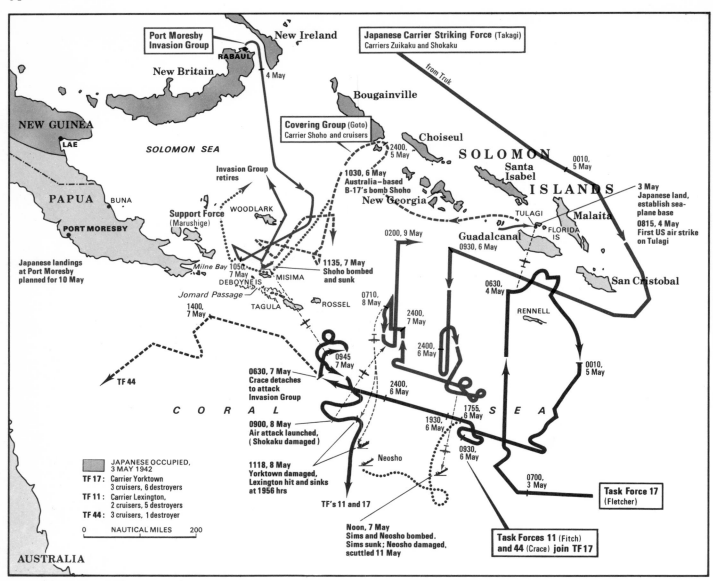

Port Moresby Invasion Group

New Ireland

Japanese Carrier Striking Force (Takagi)
Carriers Zuikaku and Shokaku

RABAUL

New Britain

4 May

Bougainville

from Truk

NEW GUINEA

LAE

SOLOMON SEA

Covering Group (Goto)
Carrier Shoho and cruisers

Choiseul

SOLOMON

0010,
5 May

2400,
5 May

Santa
Isabel

PAPUA

BUNA

Invasion Group
retires

1030, 6 May
Australia–based
B-17's bomb Shoho

New Georgia

ISLANDS

3 May
Japanese land,
establish sea-
plane base

PORT MORESBY

Support Force
(Marushige)

WOODLARK

TULAGI

Malaita

0815, 4 May
First US air strike
on Tulagi

FLORIDA
IS

Japanese landings
at Port Moresby
planned for 10 May

Milne Bay 1050,
7 May
DEBOYNE IS

MISIMA

1135, 7 May
Shoho bombed
and sunk

0200, 9 May

Guadalcanal
0930, 6 May

0630,
4 May

San Cristobal

Jomard Passage

TAGULA

ROSSEL

0710,
8 May

2400,
7 May

RENNELL

1400,
7 May

2400,
6 May

0010,
5 May

TF 44

0945
7 May

0630, 7 May
Crace detaches
to attack
Invasion Group

2400,
6 May

1755,
6 May

C O R A L

0900, 8 May
Air attack launched,
(Shokaku damaged)

2400,
6 May

1930,
6 May

S E A

1118, 8 May
Yorktown damaged,
Lexington hit and sinks
at 1956 hrs

Neosho

0930,
6 May

0700,
3 May

■ JAPANESE OCCUPIED,
3 MAY 1942

TF 17: Carrier Yorktown
3 cruisers, 6 destroyers

TF 11: Carrier Lexington,
2 cruisers, 5 destroyers

TF 44: 3 cruisers, 1 destroyer

0   NAUTICAL MILES   200

AUSTRALIA

TF's 11 and 17

Noon, 7 May
Sims and Neosho bombed.
Sims sunk; Neosho damaged,
scuttled 11 May

Task Forces 11 (Fitch)
and 44 (Crace) **join TF 17**

Task Force 17
(Fletcher)

defense of Wake. By the end of 14 December VMF-211 only had four F4F Wildcats left to do battle with. News from the outside world finally arrived on 20 December when a navy PBY flew into Wake. The aircraft brought the news that a relief expedition was being fitted out and it would only be a matter of time before they arrived. With this erroneous information, the Marines prepared to hold out until the relief arrived. On the next day, the Japanese bombers hit Wake, Wilkes and Peale with the most concentrated air bombardment so far and totally wiped out Battery D on Peale. On 21 December the remaining two aircraft on Wake took off to battle with the Japanese aircraft about to hit the atoll. It was a brave but brief fight; with only two F4Fs it was a hopeless battle against 33 bombers escorted by the far superior Zero fighters. The 2nd Lieutenant Carl Davidson attempted to dive bomb one of the bombers was shot down by a Zero. The remaining pilot, Captain Herbert Freuler, managed to shoot down one Zero but another hit his aircraft throughout the fuselage and wounded him twice. Freuler just managed to make it back to Wake before passing out from loss of blood and shock. This effectively wiped out the last of Wake's aerial power. The Americans actually set out to relieve Wake but the Japanese were quicker than their American counterparts. The *Saratoga* was still over 600 miles out from Wake when Rear Admiral Frank Fletcher stopped on 22 December to refuel his carrier. By then it was much too late for the defenders at Wake. The Japanese amphibious force was sighted at 0215 hours on 23 December and this time the Japanese would be successful in their attack. Twenty minutes later the Japanese landed simultaneously on Wake and Wilkes Islands. The landing force consisted of over 1500 crack troops.

Of this massive assault force, 100 troops hit Wilkes, 1000 men hit Wake and the rest were kept as a ready reserve. The Marines fought a gallant delaying action on the beach but stood no chance against such overwhelming odds. One by one the Marines and the civilian defenders were cut down by the Japanese. Captain Elrod and the remainder of the VMF-211 fought with their companions on the ground and although Elrod was killed while operating a Hanna gun, his action earned him the Medal of Honor. He became the first Marine aviator in World War II to be awarded the Medal

Left: The USS Lexington *suffers another internal explosion. Fire-fighting teams fought valiantly but their efforts went unrewarded.*

of Honor. The beaches were swiftly taken and the Japanese then took the small hospital. The only obstacle that kept them from advancing and taking the small airfield was Major George Potter, who was Devereux's executive officer, and 40 Marines. At 0500 hours on 23 December, Cunningham radioed Pearl Harbor: Enemy on island issue in doubt. Upon receiving this message, the acting Pacific Fleet Commander, Vice-Admiral William Pye, ordered the *Saratoga* recalled to Pearl as he feared that she would be lost. On board the *Saratoga* emotions ran high, as there was little hope now for the tiny garrison on Wake. It was only a matter of time. Finally at 0730 hours Cunningham and Devereux, after having a speedy consultation, decided to surrender as there was now no hope of relief. The last part of the battle was fought on tiny Wilkes Island where Captain Wesley Platt was in command. His Marines blocked off the access from Wake to Wilkes and were still fighting when three men were seen approaching Wake. They were Majors Devereux and Malleck and a Japanese officer. Devereux told Platt that the atoll had surrendered and the final battle was over. With the Pacific Fleet seriously damaged, US forces pushed back to the Bataan Peninsula and Corregidor, and the Japanese advancing unchecked throughout the Pacific Ocean; Wake Island's gallant resistance has been added to the proud history of the Corps.

Philippines

MacArthur's defense of the Philippines was heroic, but the resistance did not change the enemy's grand strategy. The 4th Marines, commanded by Colonel Samuel Howard, consisted of 44 officers and 728 enlisted men. They were understrength by two companies and each company was short a rifle

Above: The USS Lexington *finally goes under an hour after the destroyer* Phelps *had used five torpedoes to sink her.*

platoon. After the regiment's arrival in the Philippines, the 1st Battalion was dispatched to Mariveles at the tip of Bataan. The Marines were ordered to demolish the US Naval facilities at Cavite and Olongapo. After the destruction of Cavite by Lieutenant Colonel John Adams' 1st Separate Marine Battalion, they were ordered to transfer from Mariveles to Corregidor. They were assigned to beach defense on "The Rock." The rest of the 4th Marines crossed over in the next two nights. On 1 January 1942 the 1st Separate Battalion was redesignated as the 3rd Battalion 4th Marines.

Meanwhile the Japanese were advancing down the Bataan peninsula. On 11 March MacArthur left the Philippines, saying "I shall return." The Japanese then proceeded to speed up their offensive in Bataan. The first week of April saw the fall of Bataan and witnessed 75,000 Americans and Filipinos, including 105 Marines, begin the infamous "Bataan Death March." The siege of Corregidor began on 10 April. Constant enemy bombardment and air attacks continued for a month before they managed to land an invasion force on "The Rock" on 5 May. By noon on 6 May resistance was impossible. The Marines felt embittered that all that they had fought to achieve had come to nothing. Colonel Howard took the regimental colors and had them burned. The men of Bataan and Corregidor had put up a gallant but hopeless fight in the face of a numerically superior enemy force. It was a fight which would be remembered throughout the war. At 2400 hours Lieutenant General Jonathan Wainwright ordered the surrender of all US forces in the Philippines. The 4th Marines lost 330

Above: *The final act in the conquest of the Philippines as the Japanese lower the Stars and Stripes on Corregidor.*

Above: *A Japanese magazine celebrates the US defeat in the Philippines. After heavy fighting in the Bataan Peninsula General MacArthur left on 11 March 1942. General Wainwright announced the surrender of all US troops in the Philippines on 6 May.*

killed and 357 wounded in action. A further 239 men died in the Japanese prisoner of war camps before being liberated. Thus ended the last of the initial campaigns in which the US Marines were involved.

The next major issue of the Pacific war was the Battle of the Coral Sea. Between the 4–8 May 1942, occurred a major naval engagement which stopped the Japanese advance on Port Moresby on the southern coast of New Guinea, directly across from northern Australia. The Japanese high command hoped to isolate Australia from the USA. The Japanese naval forces were commanded by Vice-Admiral Shigeyoshi Inouye at Rabaul. Inouye

was hoping to surprise the American Fleet in the Coral Sea by launching his attack against Port Moresby. He knew that the United States could not idly stand by and watch this strategic port fall. Inouye was absolutely right but he was in for a surprise himself. Admiral Chester Nimitz knew of his plans and dispatched Task Force 11, commanded by Rear Admiral Aubrey Fitch, and Task Force 17 commanded by Rear Admiral Frank Fletcher. Also dispatched was Task Force 44 which consisted of three cruisers and one destroyer. It was not a very large naval force but it was all that was readily available, as Nimitz knew that the real danger was to come against Midway. The Japanese Carrier Striking Force was commanded by Vice-Admiral Takagi, who centered his strength around the carriers *Zuikaku* and

Shokaku. On 7 May 1942 Fletcher sent Task Force 44 to stop the Port Moresby invasion force, and he then launched his carrier-based aircraft against the Japanese strike force. That morning Takagi had also launched his aircraft and reported sighting a carrier and cruiser, but these turned out to be a destroyer, the *Sims* and the tanker *Neosho*. These were given the full treatment by the Japanese aircraft resulting in the *Sims* being sunk and the *Neosho* being scuttled on 11 May. Meanwhile aircraft from the *Lexington* had sighted the Japanese carrier *Shoho* and sank her. Inouye, not being a gambling man, then decided to order the Port Moresby invasion force back to Rabaul. The Japanese launched land-based aircraft to tackle Rear Admiral John Crace's Task Force 44 but did not inflict any damage. On 8 May Fletcher launched an attack against the *Shokaku* and scored two hits on her which put her out of action. Soon after the Japanese struck the *Lexington*, and the damage was so severe that she had to be scuttled. The *Yorktown* managed to evade any damage at all; the action was broken off and the fleet ordered to return to Pearl. The result of the battle was strategic in nature, although the Japanese inflicted heavy losses on the Americans; the Americans had succeeded in achieving their primary mission: stopping the invasion of Port Moresby, the life line to Australia. The next major battle would seal the eventual fate of the Imperial Japanese Navy.

Midway

Midway was the first major turning point in the war against Japan. Until Midway, the Japanese Imperial Fleet ranged the Pacific far and wide but that was to change very shortly. The Japanese had hit Midway with a swift destroyer attack on the night of 7 December 1941 to cover their carrier's withdrawal after clobbering Hawaii. The first Marine to be awarded the Medal of Honor in World War II was Lieutenant George Cannon, Commander of Battery H, 6th Marine Defense Battalion who was severely wounded during the attack but refused to be evacuated until his wounded men were cared for. Lieutenant Cannon died shortly after reaching the Marine first aid station from loss of blood. The swift attack against the Marine positions and airfield resulted in four men killed and 19 wounded. Midway's strength was increased over the next few weeks by VMSB-231 which flew in from Oahu; VMF-221 from the *Saratoga*, which had been recalled from Wake Island; and ground strength was increased by the arrival of elements of the 4th Marine Defense Battalion.

Admiral Chester Nimitz, Commander in Chief, Naval Forces Pacific was aware exactly where and when the Japanese would make their next move – that move would be against Midway. Navy intelligence had managed to crack the Japanese fleet code, so Nimitz was informed of the Imperial Fleet's every move. Realizing that Midway was the target of the Japanese Fleet, Nimitz recalled the *Enterprise* and *Hornet* from the South Pacific, and 19 submarines from the central Pacific. He placed his reconnaissance forces in the various approach paths to Midway. The Marine garrison was reinforced and the airfields filled to the maximum capacity. By the end of May 1942 Midway was absolutely overwhelmed with Marine and Navy aircraft. The Marines took their first decisive part in the Battle of Midway at 0616 hours, 4 June 1942. The battle was primarily a carrier action. The first wave of Japanese aircraft hit Midway installations about 0630 hours local and although outnumbered four to one, the 25 Marines fighters put up a gallant fight. These Marine pilots were led by Major Floyd Parks and Captain John Carey. The Marine did not stand a chance against the faster and more

Right: *A pall of smoke rises from the USS* Yorktown *at Midway, after she has been hit by torpedo and dive bombers.*

Imperial Japanese forces at Battle of Midway

Overall Commander was Admiral Isoroku Yamamoto aboard the *Yamato*

Advance Expeditionary Force: Commanded by Vice-Admiral Teruhisa Komatsu in the light cruiser *Katori*

No 3 Submarine Squadron:
Commanded by Rear Admiral Chimaki Kono
Submarines: I-168, I-171, I-174 and *I-175*
No 5 Submarine Squadron:
Commanded by Rear Admiral Tadashige Daigo
Submarines: I-156, I-157, I-158, I-159, I-162, I-164, I-165, and *I-166*
No 13 Submarine Squadron:
Commanded by Captain Takeharu Miyazaki
Submarines: I-121, I-122 and *I-123*
1st Carrier Striking Force: Commanded by Vice-Admiral Chuichi Nagumo
Carrier Division One: Commanded by Vice-Admiral Nagumo
Carriers: Akagi and *Kaga* (42 fighters, 51 torpedo bombers and 42 dive bombers)
Carrier Division Two: Commanded by Rear Admiral Tamon Yamaguchi
Carriers: Hiryu and *Soryu* (42 fighters, 51 torpedo bombers and 42 dive bombers)
Support Group: Commanded by Rear Admiral Hiroaki Abe
Battleships: Haruna and *Kirishima*
Heavy Cruisers: Tone and *Chikuma*
Screening Group: Commanded by Rear Admiral Susumu Kimura
Light Cruiser: Nagara
Destroyers: Akigumo, Arashi, Hagikaze, Isokaze, Hamakaze, Kazagumo, Makigumo, Maikaze, Nowaki, Tanikaze, Urakaze and *Yugumo*
Supply Ships: *Kokuyo Maru, Kyokuto Maru, Nippon Maru, Shinkoku Maru* and *Toho Maru*
Midway Occupation Group Commanded by Vice-Admiral Nobutake Kondo
Covering Group: Commanded by Vice-Admiral Nobutake Kondo
Battleships: Hiei and *Kongo*
Heavy Cruisers: Atago, Chokai, Haguro and *Myoku*
Light Cruiser: Yura
Light Carrier: Zuiho
Destroyers: Asagumo, Miegumo, Miyazuki, Murasame, Harusame, Natsugumo, Samidare and *Yudachi*

Repair Ship: Akami
Supply Ships: Genyo Maru, Kenyo Maru and *Sata* and *Tsurumi*
Support Group: Commanded by Rear Admiral Takeo Kurita
Heavy Cruisers: Kumano, Mikuma, Mogami and *Suzuya*
Destroyers: Asashio and *Arashio*
Supply Ship: Nichiei Maru
Transport Group: Commanded by Rear Admiral Raizo Tanaka composed of the Light Cruiser *Jintsu,* 12 transports, one oiler, ten destroyers and four patrol boats, and carrying 5000 crack assault troops
Seaplane Tender Group: Commanded by Rear Admiral Ruitero Fujita
Seaplane Carriers: Chitose and *Kamikawa Maru*
Destroyer: Hayashio
Patrol Boat: No 35
Northern Force: Commanded by Vice-Admiral Moshiro Hosogaya
Main Body of Northern Force:
Heavy Cruiser: Nachi
Two additional destroyers
Second Carrier Striking Force: Commanded by Rear Admiral Kakuji Kakuta
Light Carriers: Ryujo (16 fighters and 21 torpedo bombers)
Carrier: Junyo (24 fighters, and 21 dive bombers)
Heavy Cruisers: Maya and *Takao,* and three destroyers
Attu Invasion Force: Commanded by Rear Admiral Sentaro Omori
Light Cruiser: Abukuma (Flagship), four destroyers, one transport (carrying 1200 troops) and one minelayer
Main Force: Commanded by Admiral Yamamoto
Battleships: Yamato (Combined Fleet Flagship), *Nagato,* and *Mutsu*
Light Cruiser: Sendai
Light Carrier: Hosko (96 aircraft)
Destroyers: Amagiri, Asagiri, Ayanami, Fubuki, Shirayuki, Hatsuyuki, Murakumo, Isonami, Uranami, Shikinami, Yugiri, and *Shirakumo*
Seaplane Carriers: Chiyoda and *Nigshin*
Aleutain Support Force Department: Vice-Admiral Shiro Takasu
Battleships: Hyuya (Flagship), *Ise, Fuso, Yamashiro*
Light Cruisers: Oi, Kikakama
Supply Ships: Naruto, Toli Maru, San Clemte Maru and *Toa Maru*

maneuverable Zero fighters. The result of this encounter was that nine out of 12 Marine aircraft were shot down. The second section was commanded by Captain Kirk Armistead and had 13 fighters. When these initial engagements were completed, Major Parks and 14 Marine pilots were dead. The Japanese meanwhile had caused a tremendous amount of damage to the shore-based defenses on Midway. The first round went to the Japanese. Their losses were minute compared to the Americans, but Admiral Chuichi Nagumo made a decision which was to give the Americans another chance. As the Japanese aircraft returned from the attack, the senior commander stated that a further strike was necessary. A second strike of 93 aircraft was made ready to attack Midway again. This meant that all the aircraft had to be disarmed since they were ready to attack surface ships and the ordnance load was totally different. The aircraft were moved below deck and rearmed for land targets. Just as crewmen were starting to rearm, Nagumo received the long awaited news of the American surface fleet. He cancelled the rearming but it was already too late; he could not bring the aircraft to the top deck because the Midway strike aircraft were returning and the deck had to be kept clear for them to land.

While this chaos was going on, the Marines had dispatched a dive-bomber force against the Japanese fleet. These aircraft were commanded by Major Lofton Henderson (the airfield on Guadalcanal was named after him only two months later). Of these 16 aircraft only eight managed to return to Midway. Henderson was shot down but it was a very gallant attempt considering the quality of the aircraft which were at the disposal of the Marines. Fifteen B-17 bombers also attempted to strike the enemy fleet but did not cause any noticeable damage. But the finale was still to come; carrier-based planes from the *Enterprise* and *Yorktown* hit the enemy fleet where it hurt most. They sank three of the four carriers: the *Akagi*, *Soryu* and *Kaga*,

and later that evening aircraft from the *Enterprise* severely damaged the remaining *Hiryu*. On 5 June 12 Marine bombers from Midway, commanded by Captain Marshall Tyler, attacked two of the enemy's damaged cruisers. One Marine aviator, Captain Richard Fleming earned the Medal of Honor by crashing his burning aircraft directly into an after turret of the cruiser *Mikuma*.

To sum up the battle, it was a total victory for the United States and a disaster for the Imperial Japanese Navy, although they were not to be counted out as yet. Marine losses for the battle were 49 men killed in action and 53 wounded. This was the last defensive action which the Marines took part in during World War II.

Above: *The USS* Yorktown *retaliates with anti-aircraft fire during the Battle of Midway.*
Left: *The* Yorktown *lists badly as destroyers of the* Porter *Class come alongside.*
Below: *The* Yorktown *lies dead in the water as fire control parties try desperately to save "Old Yorky."*

Carrier Force commanded by Rear Admiral Fletcher

Task Force 16: Commanded by Rear Admiral Raymond A Spruance
Carriers: Enterprise (27 fighters, 19 bombers, 14 torpedo bombers, 19 scout planes)
Hornet (27 fighters, 19 bombers, 15 torpedo bombers, and 18 scout planes)
Cruisers: Atlanta, Minneapolis, New Orleans, Northampton, Pensacola and *Vincennes*
Destroyers: Alywin, Balck, Coryngham, Benham, Ellet, Maury, Monaghan, Phelps and *Worden*
Supply Ships: Cimmarron, Dewey, Monssen and *Platte*
Task Force 17: Commanded by Rear Admiral Frank J Fletcher
Carriers: Yorktown (25 fighters, 19 bombers, 14 torpedo bombers and 19 scout planes)
Cruisers: Astoria and *Portland*
Destroyers: Anderson, Gwin, Hammond, Hughes, Morris and *Russell*
Submarines were under the operational control of Rear Admiral Robert H English at Pearl Harbor
Midway Patrol Group: Cachalot, Cuttlefish, Dolphin, Flying Fish, Gato, Grayling, Grenadier, Gugeon, Grouper, Nautilus and *Tambor* and *Trout*
North of Oahu Patrol: Finback, Growler, Pike and *Tarpon*
Reconnaissance Group: Narwhal, Plunger and *Trigger*

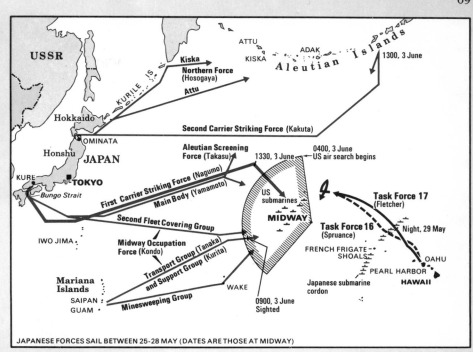

JAPANESE FORCES SAIL BETWEEN 25-28 MAY (DATES ARE THOSE AT MIDWAY)

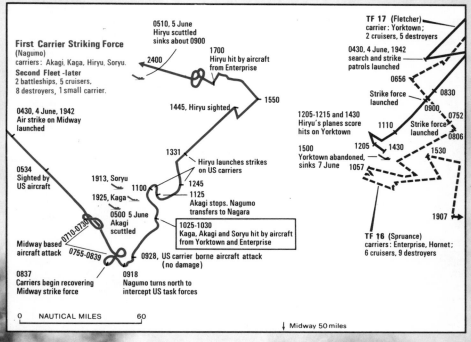

Badly needed reinforcements land at Guadalcanal to join the US Marines in their attempt to drive the Japanese off this obscure island in the Solomons. For many Marines Guadalcanal was their first taste of action in World War II.

Their Finest Hour

Guadalcanal

Immediately after the Battle of Midway, the central point of the war in the Pacific moved back to the Southwest Pacific Area again. The Japanese wished to strengthen their hold in that area, and decided to temporarily give up the plan to disrupt communications between the Australians and Americans. Japanese planners decided on a two-fold maneuver, beginning with an overland campaign from the north coast of New Guinea to capture the vital supply base at Port Moresby, and at the same time consolidating their position in the Solomons.

Meanwhile American interest in the southern Solomons was picking up considerably. The two overall commanders were Admiral Chester Nimitz and General Douglas MacArthur, men who were not used to being on the defensive. Pressure was now off Hawaii and the time was ripe for offensive action. The important question was where to strike and who would command the offensive. This was settled by a Joint Chiefs of Staff directive on 2 July 1942, ordering a parallel advance upon Rabaul, up the Solomons and along the New Guinea coast. It was to be accomplished in three stages: the seizure of the Santa Cruz Islands, then Tulagi and the adjacent islands; the occupation of the Solomons, with Papua and New Guinea up to the Huon Peninsula;

finally, the capture of Rabaul and the remainder of the Bismarck Archipelago. The initial phase of this operation was code named "Watchtower." Also the boundary between the Southwest Pacific and Pacific Ocean Commands was moved slightly so that Guadalcanal came under Nimitz's sphere of operational control. MacArthur was to oversee the completion of the final two phases.

On 5 July 1942 reconnaissance aircraft confirmed the reports of the Australian coastwatchers that the Japanese had transferred large troop concentrations from Tulagi to the nearby island of Guadalcanal and were building an airfield of unknown proportions. If the Japanese were allowed to complete this airfield unopposed, they would be able to launch fighters and bombers at all Allied attempts to move into the Solomons and the Coral Sea. The all-important objective was now to seize Guadalcanal and the strategic airstrip at Lunga Point, later to be renamed Henderson Field, and consequently the Santa Cruz portion was dropped from the agenda. A major reason for killing the Santa Cruz operation was that the island was extremely malarial – and personnel losses would have been very high. Guadalcanal itself was no paradise as the Marines who fought and died there could attest.

Ninety miles long and 25 miles wide, a mixture of rain forests, stinking malarial swamps, thick grasslands and undergrowth, and steep, treacherous

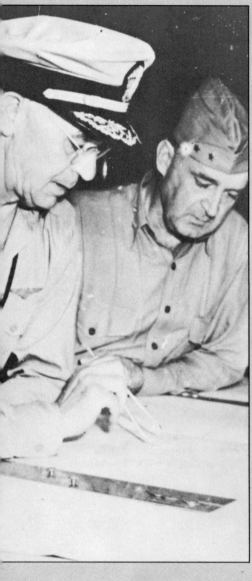

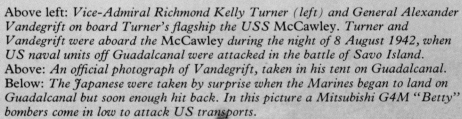

Above left: *Vice-Admiral Richmond Kelly Turner (left) and General Alexander Vandegrift on board Turner's flagship the USS McCawley. Turner and Vandegrift were aboard the McCawley during the night of 8 August 1942, when US naval units off Guadalcanal were attacked in the battle of Savo Island.*
Above: *An official photograph of Vandegrift, taken in his tent on Guadalcanal.*
Below: *The Japanese were taken by surprise when the Marines began to land on Guadalcanal but soon enough hit back. In this picture a Mitsubishi G4M "Betty" bombers come in low to attack US transports.*

Edson's raiders who landed on Tanambogo and Gavutu Island encountered much stiffer resistance than the main landing at Lunga Point on Guadalcanal. By 8 August Edson's men had moved on to Tulagi and all resistance had been overcome.

mountains; that was Guadalcanal, a strategic objective for a few months on a general's map which later as the war progressed would be forgotten and returned to its semi-primeval state of existence. The "Canal," as it became known to the Marines, was situated in the southern half of the Solomons group, which comprises a large

Below: *Marine anti-aircraft personnel on the USS* Wasp *during a lull. The* Wasp *covered the landings for the first day and then withdrew.*

number of islands running for 600 miles in a southeast direction from Rabaul, Buka and Bougainville. The remaining islands and atolls form a double chain separated by a deep channel which was given the name of "The Slot."

In the weeks which followed, plans were finalized, differences settled, troops gathered and an overall strategic commander selected. The amphibious force was commanded by Rear Admiral Richmond Kelly Turner and an air support force under Rear Admiral

Above: *Crewmen load a 500-lb demolition bomb on an SBD Dauntless, which is being prepared for take off from the* Enterprise, *7 August 1942.*

Noyes. Rear Admiral Frank Fletcher, who commanded the carrier task force at the Battles of the Coral Sea and Midway, was in tactical control of the entire operation. The air support force was composed of the carriers *Enterprise*, *Saratoga* and *Wasp* supported by the brand-new battleship *North Carolina*, six cruisers and a substantial number of destroyers. The convoy consisted of four cruisers and 11 destroyers, and was carrying the 1st US Marine Division (composed of the 1st, 5th and 11th Regiments, but minus the 7th Regiment), and the 2nd Marine Regiment, 2nd Marine Division. The Marine force was commanded by a crusty old fighter, Major General Alexander Archer Vandegrift. The convoy was screened by Rear Admiral Victor Crutchley with a force of three Australian cruisers and one American (HMAS *Australia*, *Canberra* and *Hobart*, and USS *Chicago*). The 19 transports which were carrying the 19,000 men were provided with as much support as could be mustered for an enterprise of such an extremely important nature. The operation was being supported by land-based aircraft from airfields in Fiji, New Caledonia and New Hebrides, and also from army aircraft under MacArthur's command.

There were to be two landings, the first on the larger island of Guadalcanal and the second on the much smaller island of Tulagi.

The amphibious force left Wellington, New Zealand, on 22 July and met the air support task force south of Fiji; after a four-day practice on a remote island of the group, they set sail for the "Canal" on 31 July. The force was undetected in its approach because of heavy haze and intermittent rain squalls. On 7 August the initial landings were made on Guadalcanal near Lunga Point and at Tulagi. Both were highly successful, as there was no opposition at Guadalcanal, and by nightfall 11,000 Marines were ashore. On the next day the airfield was secured and the Marines were putting out scouts to ascertain what the Japanese were planning. The Tulagi situation was not as clear-cut, the Japanese were better prepared, and the three battalions of Marines met stiff resistance. By 8 August Tulagi was completely under Marine control, the casualties were 108 Marines dead and 140 wounded. The Japanese garrison of 1500 troops was practically exterminated to a man. Meanwhile it had taken only 48 hours to gain the initial foothold on the "Canal," but it would be another six months of intense and bitter fighting before it could be secured. The scene was now set for one of the hardest fought campaigns in the history of the US Marine Corps.

Japanese actions were swift: immediately after the US landings, a striking force from the 25th Air Flotilla was dispatched from Rabaul. On 7 and 8 August Japanese bombers attacked the transports lying off Lunga Point and would have caused heavy damage, except for the timely warnings given by the Australian coastwatchers. The attacks were intercepted by US aircraft from the naval carriers but two destroyers were hit and one transport became a total loss. The Marines were digging in around Henderson Field and prepared for a major Japanese attack.

When the news reached Rabaul, Admiral Gunichi Mikawa was in the middle of preparing a major offensive against Port Moresby. He immediately realized what the Americans were attempting and decided to send all available ships to attack and destroy the US naval forces off Guadalcanal, and then reinforce and exterminate the Marine landing force on the island. By 7 August five heavy and two light cruisers were sailing toward the "Canal." To make matters worse, Imperial General Headquarters issued orders to reinforce the garrison of the island and a convoy carrying 500 additional troops, escorted by de-

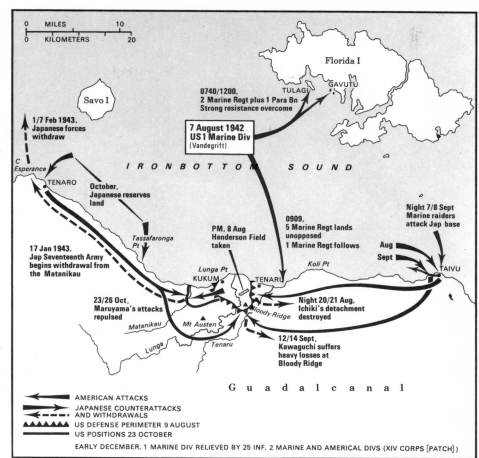

stroyers were en route. But shortly after sailing one of the transports was torpedoed by an American submarine which resulted in the convoy being recalled to Rabaul.

On the beach itself, the supply and logistics problems were mounting for Vandegrift, who was trying to keep to his original timetable. At 1400 hours he ordered the 1st Battalion 5th Marines to advance westwards to Alligator Creek and dig in for the night. By 1600 hours Vandegrift was ashore and had established his forward command post. During all this the Japanese were far from idle; they had launched two air strikes. The first was at 1320 hours and consisted of 24 aircraft of the Japanese 25th Air Flotilla. Warning was received from an Australian Coastwatcher and a welcoming party was arranged. Twelve Japanese aircraft were shot down by Wildcats from the *Saratoga*, but the USS *Mugford*, a destroyer was hit and 22 men killed. Two hours later there was an attack by ten Aichi 99 dive bombers but no serious damage was recorded. The First Marine Combat Group B, commanded by Colonel Clifton Cates, had been ordered by Vandegrift to proceed to Mount Austen but they were held up because of the terrific heat and tropical undergrowth. Vandegrift realized that Mount Austen would not be reached that day; so he changed his plans accordingly. The Marines were to secure their positions and dig in for

the night. The next morning the Marines would push forward toward Lunga and by-pass Mount Austen, occupying the airstrip from the south. The 5th Marines were to advance on Lunga also and then continue to Kukum. There were many shaky Marines on the first night but the Japanese did not mount the expected counterattack. On Saturday, 8 August, the 1st Battalion, 5th Marines, supported by the 1st Tank Battalion, succeeded in crossing over the mouth of Alligator Creek. The Marines believed that this was in fact the Tenaru River, but in reality it was the Ilu. The 1st Battalion, 1st Marines, acting on orders swung west away from Mount Austen and began to advance. This unit moved very slowly and had trouble crossing one of the numerous creeks in its path. The other units, the 2nd and 3rd Battalions, made faster progress through the jungle than their counterparts in the 1st. The day was extremely hot and humid. By the end of the day the 1st Battalion had passed the airfield, but the 2nd and 3rd Battalions had in their turn slowed down and were still south of the airfield when the order came to dig in for the night.

The 5th Marines made good progress and managed to take a few Japanese prisoners. It was gathered from information sweated out of the enemy that no Japanese resistance would be encountered within the next 48 hours. Vandegrift took immediate

Above: *US transports evacuate Tulagi on 10 August 1942, leaving behind the experienced Edson's Raiders.*

Above: *Marines set out in their rafts for the beaches at Lunga Point, during the initial landings on Guadalcanal. They met no resistance on the beaches in this, the first Marine amphibious operation in World War II.*

advantage of this situation and ordered the 5th Marines to advance more rapidly. The regiment crossed the Lunga over the main bridge, and by skirting the airfield to the north, it took Kukum along with large quantities of supplies.

Meanwhile things on the beach were not going according to plans and after another attack by Japanese Betty bombers, escorted by Zero fighters, Fletcher's fighter strength was being gradually thinned down. From 99 aircraft, he was now down to 78 and was also dangerously low on fuel reserves. Fletcher decided that he was putting his entire Task Force 61 in jeopardy if he remained off Guadalcanal any longer and asked Ghormley for permission to withdraw his carriers. Ghormley was not pleased with this request but because he was too far removed from the scene, felt that it would be unreasonable to deny a request made in such an urgent manner. This decision was the most controversial made during the entire Guadalcanal campaign: the main points being that only 50 percent of the supplies for the Marine force had been

Below: *The transport USS* President Jackson *turns to avoid Japanese attacks off Guadalcanal on 12 November 1942. The background smoke comes from a Japanese aircraft which had crashed into the USS* San Francisco.

Above: *Marines comb a pine grove on Guadalcanal in search of snipers on 5 September 1942.*

unloaded; Fletcher still had enough fuel for at least 72 hours; the Japanese air attacks had been beaten off; and the majority of ships were undamaged. Also unbeknown Mikawa was steaming down "The Slot" making for Guadalcanal. US aircraft had sighted the Japanese squadron on the evening of the 7th but due to a belated report, coupled with erroneous information and bad weather, the enemy was not located again that day. Therefore, Mikawa was able to make his approach down "The Slot" undetected.

Below: *Marines start preparing a rough air strip shortly after landing.*

Turner summoned Rear Admiral Crutchley and Major General Vandegrift aboard his flagship the USS *McCawley*, and relayed the information to them that Fletcher was pulling out and taking their air cover and supplies with him. Vandegrift's exact words were not recorded. While Turner was expanding on the details, Mikawa's force sailed right past the picket destroyers and turned their guns to bear point blank at the unsuspecting *Canberra* and *Chicago*. The *Canberra* was hit so hard that she had to be abandoned but the *Chicago* was more fortunate, and received no crippling damage. The Japanese did not wait to see the result of their surprise attack but sailed out of range and toward the northern patrol group. The southern patrol group was completely dis-

oriented and no warning was sent to the northern group. The northern group fared even worse than its southern counterparts. The Japanese sunk the USS *Astoria*, *Vincennes* and *Quincy* in less than an hour. Mikawa had taken the US Navy by surprise and the result was an astounding victory which would have been even better if he had taken the initiative to destroy the transports left unprotected. It is only conjecture but the entire campaign on "The Canal" would have changed, and possibly the war in the Pacific would have taken a different turn if the transports had been eliminated.

This disaster confirmed Fletcher's belief that he must remove his Task Force from the danger zone. The 9 August was spent in preparation for departure and by sunset Task Force 61 was steaming away. The Marines under Vandegrift were now completely on their own. The situation was not very inviting. The US Navy had lost control of the seas around the Solomons. The nearest air support was in Espiritu Santo in the New Hebrides. Supplies were already starting to run out, and morale was not very high after what most Marines thought was outright naval desertion. Vandegrift realized that he was in no position to attack, so his schedule stressed defense. His most important operational concern was to make the airstrip functional at all costs. An extended perimeter defense was established round the airfield. The Marines set up .30 and .50 caliber machine guns, backed up by 37mm guns and 90mm AA guns all around the defensive perimeter. The feeling of being abandoned was considerably lessened on 14 August when the Navy ran the gauntlet of enemy aircraft and surface ships to bring supplies of ammunition and fuel, as well as bare essentials to the Marines at Guadalcanal. Vandegrift decided to make a small foray against the Japanese by driving them across the Matanikau. This action was successful but did not allay the doubts in his mind of the ability of his men to sustain and repulse a heavy attack from the numerically superior Japanese force on the island. The major thing which aided the Marines was the Japanese confusion over exactly what to do – the Japanese believed that the US would eventually get tired of the "insignificant" island and withdraw. Japanese intelligence showed that the Marines were digging in and this put a whole new picture on the screen. Plans were drawn up to expel the Marines from Guadalcanal.

Right: *Marines move through the inhospitable jungle growth of Guadalcanal charting unmapped territory.*

82

Below left: *Japanese soldiers killed during the Battle of Bloody Ridge, 13–14 September 1942. Japanese dead totalled over 700.*
Below: *Routine patrols on "The Canal."*
Right: *A Marine gun crew prepare a 90 mm anti-aircraft gun for action.*

Lieutenant General Haruyoshi Hyakutake, the 17th Army Commander, was ordered to retake Tulagi and Guadalcanal before setting out on the all important mission of securing Port Moresby. Hyakutake had over 50,000 men in his 17th Army but he had a slight problem – they were spread out all over the Pacific. Undaunted, he believed that if he could send one expert unit into the islands then the Marine force could be driven into the sea and utterly destroyed. He chose Colonel Kiyanao Ichiki's 28th Infantry from Guam to accomplish the task. At the time he appeared to be the ideal man for the task at hand but events proved him to be impetuous and rash. On 18 August he was to take 900 men on six destroyers and land at Taivu Point, around 20 miles from the Marine positions. The remainder of his 2500 men outfit would join him within the week.

Vandegrift was being kept up to date by his native coastwatchers and knew that Japanese forces were building up in the east. Captain Charles Brush set out on a patrol on 19 August with Marines of Abel Company, 1st Marines, heading toward Koli Point. At noon Japanese troops were sighted,

Brush sent his executive officer, Lieutenant Joseph Jachym, around to flank them and put them in a cross fire between the two Marine columns. The result was 31 out of 35 Japanese dead. From the documents and maps taken from the bodies it was discovered that they were army personnel and not navy who had previously been fighting the Marines on Guadalcanal.

Ichiki attacked the Marine positions on the mouth of Alligator Creek on the Ilu River (still called erroneously the Tenaru) early on 21 August. He recklessly decided that the 900 men he

Left: *Always prepared for action in Guadalcanal, this Marine has his grenades near at hand while he gazes at his sweetheart's picture.*
Below: *A B-17 Flying Fortress swoops over the jungle of Guadalcanal.*

had brought with him would be sufficient and he need not wait for the rest of his 2500-man force. The Japanese made two attempts: the first at 0240 hours and the second at 0500 hours, both attacks were repulsed with heavy casualties to the attackers. Some of the Japanese were caught on the far bank of the river and Colonel Gerald Thomas, Divisional Operations Officer, recommended to Vandegrift to counterattack immediately and drive the survivors into the sea. Vandegrift ordered the reserve battalion, Cate's 1st Battalion 1st Marines under Lieutenant Colonel Creswell to cross the river and drive downstream all Japanese troops. Meanwhile Pollock's men provided a heavy and continuous fire from the other side of the river. Also to ensure total success a platoon of light tanks was brought up and Marine

aircraft would be utilized to strafe the entire affected area. Needless to say, the operation was a complete success. In Vandegrift's own words "the rear of the tanks looked like meat grinders." By 1700 hours, the Battle of Tenaru (Ilu) was finished. The Marines had killed over 800 Japanese, taken 15 prisoners and of the survivors, most of these died in the jungle. Colonel Ichiki survived the battle but upon reaching Taivu shot himself after burning his regimental colors.

The Battle of Tenaru was an American victory but there was still a great deal to be done before Vandegrift's position on Guadalcanal could be called secure. The Japanese became even more determined to drive the Marines off the island. To make the airfield serviceable, US Marine Corps engineers utilized captured Japanese equipment, as their own was still on board the transports. On 12 August the aide to Rear Admiral John McCain flew a Catalina flying boat onto the airfield for an inspection of the runway. McCain was responsible for land-based air operations. The strip was only 2600 feet long, with no drainage and no steel matting covers, and there were no taxiways. The aide was a realistic man and passed the field as fit for fighter aircraft operations. The airfield was named Henderson Field after a hero of the Battle of Midway. The first aircraft arrived on 20 August: 12 Dauntless dive bombers commanded by Major Richard Mangrum and 19 Marine Wildcat fighters under Captain John Smith.

The Japanese had gathered two task forces consisting of three aircraft carriers, eight battleships, four heavy cruisers, two light cruisers, 21 destroyers and other vessels, with air cover provided by the 25th Air Flotilla at Rabaul. To meet this small armada, Fletcher had at his disposal three

aircraft carriers, one battleship, four cruisers and ten destroyers. The resulting battle became known as the Battle of the Eastern Solomons and was very like Midway, though the result was a stalemate. Dogfights became part of the Marines' daily routine. But without these pilots and support crews of the "Cactus Air Force" as it became known, Vandegrift's Marines might not have held their beach-head in the black days of August and September 1942. These Marine pilots lived in tents and dug-outs, eating rice and spam as a staple diet but they were the actual front line of resistance at the "Canal." However, at the beginning of September, Vandegrift's position was not very reassuring. His battle-weary troops were hungry, stricken with dysentery and jungle rot, and by October malaria would also take its toll. The Marines could not get an uninterrupted night's sleep because of the Japanese night prowler aircraft nicknamed "Louie the Louse" and "Washing Machine Charlie." All this was beginning to take its toll on the men, and they had to wait for the Japanese to act.

Admiral Raizo Tanaka managed time after time to run the gauntlet with night-time runs to reinforce Guadalcanal. This became so regular that the Marines called it "The Tokyo Express." Vandegrift was in sore need of reinforcements because the Japanese were landing more and more troops to both the east and west of his perimeter. He transferred troops from Tulagi to Guadalcanal, including the experienced Edson's Raiders. The Marines made occasional thrusts into the Japanese-held areas to keep the enemy

Below: *The USS* Enterprise *loses another SBD Dauntless from her decks following a violent internal explosion during the Battle of Vera Cruz.*

on their toes and to gather intelligence information. On 10 September one of Vandegrift's urgent requests was granted: down to only 11 out of the original 38 Wildcats, Ghormley sent an immediate 24 replacements. Colonel Edson moved his command post and his mixed force of raiders and parachutists to a ridge one mile south of Henderson Field and not far from Vandegrift's own headquarters. This ridge was 1000 yards long, running northwest to southeast and surrounded by steep slopes and dense jungle growth. This was to be renamed in a few days "Bloody Ridge."

Edson deployed his 700 men in the prime locations for a possible Japanese penetration attempt. Jungle was cleared out and barbed wire strung out between the trees to give it a semblance of a perimeter. In direct support of Edson's men were 105mm howitzers and the 2nd Marine Battalion 5th Marines. The 12 September brought the long-awaited Japanese attack. It started off with an intense naval bombardment of the Marine positions, followed up immediately by heavy mortar and artillery and then an all-out infantry attack by Kawaguchi's troops. The Marines were displaced from their positions but through faulty communications and the disorientation of their men the Japanese attack lost impetus and stopped. The Marines under Edson then charged and retook their former positions along the ridge. Now the long process of digging in began again, with more barbed wire laid down and preparations for the next attack which would surely come. The noise was intense, with naval bombardment, artillery and mortar barrages and the follow-up infantry, but Kawaguchi threw 2000 men across

Below: *In an earlier action off Santa Cruz Island on 15 September 1942, the* Wasp *was torpedoed by a Japanese submarine. She was so badly damaged that she had to be abandoned and was sunk later that day.*

the slope on 13 September. The massive wave of men was something the Marines had never experienced before. As fast as they cut the Japanese down, their comrades climbed over the dead bodies. The Marines were at the breaking point when "Red Mike" Edson took the front himself and urged his weary men to smoke down all the enemy. Edson called for increased artillery support and practically brought it down onto his own positions. Another stalwart was Major Kenneth Bailey who kept shouting the traditional Marine Corps cry "Do you want to live forever." Between the intense and accurate fire coming from the Marines on the ridge and the

Top: *The crew of 1.1-inch guns are ready for action on board the USS* San Juan *at Santa Cruz.*
Above: *Anti-aircraft shells burst over the USS* Hornet *at the height of the Battle at Santa Cruz.*

perfect artillery support, the Japanese were being decimated. By 14 September the Japanese were defeated and Kawaguchi knew it. The remainder of his force retreated to Matanikau. The Japanese dead totalled over 700 with an additional 600 wounded. US casualties were 59 dead and 204 wounded. The US Marines had achieved another total victory but this was to be overshadowed again by a defeat at sea.

Above: *A destroyer evacuates survivors from the crippled carrier Hornet. She was eventually sunk by Japanese "Long Lance" torpedoes after US destroyers had failed to scuttle her.*

Above: *Navy transports at anchor off Guadalcanal on 4 November 1942. By this time Vandegrift was receiving supplies more regularly than he had done in August.*
Below: *Japanese transports, part of the "Tokyo Express," burn after having been beached during the two-day naval Battle of Guadalcanal.*

Admiral Turner kept his word and rushed reinforcements to Guadalcanal – the 7th Marines whom he had picked up at the New Hebrides after their stint of duty at Samoa. The task force and its carrier escort force were sighted on 14 September by a Japanese aircraft. Turner remained on course until nightfall and then withdrew the *McCawley* and the six precious transports with their cargo of 4000 Marines. The carriers *Hornet* and *Wasp*, the battleship *North Carolina* and various escort destroyers continued on course. On 15 September at 0220 hours, the Japanese submarines *I-15* and *I-19* attacked the carrier force. The result of this attack was devastating: the *Wasp* was abandoned and sunk by the

Lansdowne, the *North Carolina* had a 30 by 18 foot gaping hole put in its side below the waterline and the destroyer *O'Brien* was also sunk. This naval action occurred off the Santa Cruz islands and again the US Navy had suffered another cruel blow from the Imperial Navy. Turner's decision to withdraw was vindicated by his safe arrival at Guadalcanal and the landing of the 4000 men and some supplies. There was a brief lull in the fighting while both sides experimented and probed with the enemy's defensive positions. The Marines lost a few skirmishes and won a few but it was not until November that the offensive really got under way. The US was determined not to lose its hold on

Guadalcanal. But as the struggle reached its climax, President Roosevelt ordered the Chiefs of Staff to send all available equipment, supplies and troops to the two priority theaters – the Pacific and North African – even if this meant drastically reducing strategic commitments elsewhere. Admiral King, CNO, could not send any carriers to the South Pacific, but he diverted a sizeable force to SOPAC, including a battleship, six cruisers, 24 submarines and 130 naval aircraft. General George Marshall, Army Chief of Staff, also sent an additional force of 75 army aircraft from Hawaii to reinforce the southwest Pacific but would not increase the troop commitment to the area, especially with the

Above: *The Japanese on Guadalcanal suffered appalling casualties. They were as short of supplies as the US and also suffered from malaria.*
Below: *By November Marines of the 2nd Raider Battalion were conducting operations on the southern shore of Guadalcanal.*

pressure on from Operation Torch, the Allied landings in North Africa. However reinforcements were stripped from the other island bases and sent to the "Canal." On 4 November two regiments from the 2nd Marine Division were landed and a further 6000 officers and men were landed on 6 November from Noumea and Espiritu Santo (the latter were troops of the American Division). The two convoys were commanded by Rear Admiral Turner and were escorted by two squadrons, the first under Rear Admiral Nicholas Scott and the second under Rear Admiral Daniel Callaghan. This force was shadowed by a task force formed around the hastily refitted *Enterprise* and the two battleships *Washington* and *South Dakota*. The Japanese were still no less determined than the US Marines to gain complete control of Guadalcanal, and November saw another major attempt to reinforce the island and force the Marines to abandon it. Their plan was in no way different from those of their previous attempts. Bombardment of Henderson Field by two naval squadrons, followed up by artillery and mortar fire and a massive infantry breakthrough. The only difference this time was that a third squadron was escorting the rest of the 38th Division from Rabaul, while a fourth squadron gave support. This was by far the largest planned general offensive to date.

Unknowingly, the US convoy, escorted by Rear Admiral Scott's squadron, arrived off Lunga Point early on 11 November and was joined by Callaghan's squadron on 12 November. Just a few hours later, a strong Japanese naval force including the battleships *Hiei* and *Kirishima* was sighted steaming down "The Slot." Turner, nonplussed, calmly finished unloading the transports of all troops and supplies and then sailed in convoy for Espiritu Santo, escorted by only three destroyers. The remainder of the combined escort forces commanded by Rear Admiral Callaghan stayed behind to engage the enemy fleet; although outnumbered by superior Japanese forces, he did so to cover Turner's withdrawal.

After escorting the transports clear of the anchorage, Callaghan steered west to engage the enemy. It was an extremely dark and dismal night with no moon. In the early hours of the morning of 13 November, both forces practically collided before opening fire. The battle which followed lasted only 24 minutes and must go on record for being one of the most furious sea engagements ever fought. The Japanese lost two destroyers and the battleship *Hiei* was critically damaged and left dead in the water for the US aircraft to finish off the next day. The US task force lost two light cruisers and four destroyers; both Rear Admirals Callaghan and Scott were killed in the battle and casualties were heavy. Callaghan's action accomplished his main objective allowing the task force time to intervene. The following afternoon, naval aircraft from the carrier *Enterprise* sank a cruiser and severely damaged other surface ships of the Japanese cruiser bombardment force. Furthermore, aircraft from Henderson Field inflicted grave damage to the transports unloading on the north side of the island and sunk seven out of 11. The Japanese heavy bombardment force was now reorganized and reinforced to cover the transports. It was composed of the battleship *Kirishima*, four cruisers and nine destroyers. Vice-Admiral William Halsey, who had relieved Ghormley on 18 October, sent Rear Admiral Willis Lee with the battleships *Washington* and *South Dakota*, and four destroyers to attack it. Lee led his small squadron around the southeast tip of Guadalcanal and immediately after midnight engaged the enemy in the narrow channel south of Savo Island. This battle was fought at a longer range than the preceeding one, but the fighting was just as intense. The *Kirishima* was so heavily

damaged that she had to be scuttled; and one Japanese and three US destroyers had been sunk. The *South Dakota* was damaged but remained afloat. At daylight on 15 November the four remaining Japanese transports were spotted by the Marines aground and helpless; shore batteries opened up and aided by aircraft from Henderson Field turned them into blazing hulks. Out of 10,000 troops which sailed with the ill-fated expedition, only 4000 arrived and they were without equipment or rations. Despite its heavy losses the two-day battle of Guadalcanal was a victory for the US Navy.

At the end of November the Japanese tried once more to reinforce Guadalcanal, but Halsey sent out a squadron of five cruisers and four destroyers to intercept it. On 30 November this cruiser squadron encountered eight Japanese destroyers attempting to bring supplies and reinforcements to the garrison at Tassafaronga. Only one Japanese destroyer was sunk, but the US Navy had four of its cruisers hit by

Left: *As the sun rises in December 1942, the bodies of Japanese soldiers are revealed in the mud-swollen banks of the Tenaru River.*
Below: *Marines use dirt and chemicals to save a precious Grumman "Wildcat" on Henderson Field.*

Above: *2nd Lieutenant Mitchell Paige of the 7th Marines receives his Congressional Medal of Honor for Gallantry from General Vandegrift.*

torpedoes. This was the last of the midnight encounters in the narrow waters of the South Solomons. On the last day of 1942 Japanese Imperial General Headquarters decided to abandon Guadalcanal and fall back to a line of defense based on New Georgia. On 9 December General Alexander Patch relieved Vandegrift and during the next two months the 1st Marine Division was withdrawn for a much needed rest and refit to Australia. It was relieved by the 25th US Division on 31 December. On 4 January 1943

the 2nd Marine Division Headquarters and 6th Marine Regiment arrived from New Zealand bringing the strength of the Guadalcanal garrison to 50,000 men. The Japanese on the other hand were down to 25,000 effectives. They were underfed and disease ridden, but were still willing to fight to the last man. General Imamura, Commander in Chief, 8th Area Army, ordered them to Cape Esperance, from where they were all to be evacuated during the first week in February. Exactly six months after the first US Marines landed at Red Beach on Guadalcanal, the last Japanese had been safely evacuated from "The Canal." General Patch was left in undisputed control of the island. Fortitude, courage, failure to give in and belief in victory carried the Marines through one of the most arduous campaigns of their history.

General George Marshall, Army Chief of Staff, summed it up well by saying: "The resolute defense of these Marines and the desperate gallantry of our naval task forces marked the turning in the Pacific." The US Marines who served on "The Canal" made up a little doggerel which summed up their feelings exactly:

And when he gets to heaven
To St Peter he will tell:
"One more Marine reporting, sir –
I've served my time in Hell!"

The 3rd Marines stagger onto Guam during the landings on 21 July 1944. This operation had to be postponed for a month because Japanese resistance on the neighboring islands Saipan and Tinian was too fierce.

The Amphibious Machine

Rabaul

The next major objective for the US commanders was Rabaul, the Japanese stronghold at the eastern end of New Britain. Rabaul had been taken by the Japanese at the outset of the war. It was subjected to heavy air attacks from the Japanese main base at Truk and, to make matters worse, from Admiral Nagumo's carrier force. On 23 January 1942 Japanese assault troops landed at Rabaul, New Britain and at Kavieng, New Ireland. The extremely small Australian garrison stood absolutely no chance whatsoever against the Japanese force. Rabaul was turned into a main Japanese support base capable of handling 100,000 men and 600 aircraft. The Japanese stationed their Eighth Fleet there and built superb defenses consisting of mines, cement blocks and hidden machine-gun positions. The American strategy was not to attack Rabaul directly but to isolate it from the main war effort. As long as they retained this massive installation, they would be a thorn in the flesh of the

Allies. They would be able to dispatch aircraft and naval vessels to destroy any Allied landing attempts. Nimitz could not break out into the Central Pacific; and MacArthur could not break out by advancing along the northern coast of New Guinea. The first significant operation was to advance up the Solomons and seize the enemy base at Munda Point on the northeast end of New Georgia. This entire operation was badly planned and mismanaged. It required not one but five amphibious landings, and over a month's hard fighting. By the end of the campaign, the Marines had lost 128 killed and 307 wounded in action. The main aim had been to occupy the Russell Islands as an air and naval base and then advance on New Georgia, ultimately raking Munda Point and its airfield. On 21 February 1943 the US 43rd Infantry Division landed on the Russell Islands and discovered that the islands had no enemy garrison. Halsey's fleet continued to put constant pressure on the Japanese shipping and was now in a position to do something about the Japanese raiding down "The Slot."

Admiral Yamamoto, Commander of the Combined Fleet sent his aircraft carriers to challenge US air superiority openly but was himself shot down on 18 April on his way to Bougainville. Japanese morale took a nosedive with the loss of their greatest naval commander. The actual campaign to neutralize Rabaul would take over 10 months. The most important amphibious operations during this phase were: New Georgia, Bougainville and Cape Gloucester. However, before the Allies could think about tackling Rabaul, Guadalcanal had to be neutralized and controlled. This was made much easier when the Marines brought in the new F4U Corsairs. On 7 April 1943 76 fighters from the "Cactus Air

Above: *Marine experts train units of the 160th Infantry, 40th Division in amphibious landings at the scene of the Marines' first victory at Guadalcanal.*
Below: *Members of a Marine Parachute Regiment leave Guadalcanal to assist operations on Vella Lavella, an island further up the Solomon chain.*

Above: *Lieutenant General Haruyoshi Hyakutake, Commander of the 17th Army, directed all land operations in the Solomons from his headquarters at Rabaul. This picture was taken after he had surrendered at the end of the war.*

Force" at Henderson Field shot down 39 out of 160 enemy aircraft. On his first flight 1st Lieutenant James E Swett engaged and shot down seven Japanese dive bombers. The final air assault over Guadalcanal climaxed in June, when a force of 120 enemy aircraft was, for all practical purposes, annihilated.

The New Georgia campaign was initiated on the 21 June when O and P Companies, 4th Raider Battalion landed at Segi Point, at the southern portion of New Georgia. After rescuing an Australian coastwatcher, the raiders advanced on the 3-inch coastal battery at Viru Harbor. The raiders had to eliminate this coastal battery because an army landing was imminent and if the guns were not silenced there would be dead infantrymen on the beaches. The raiders commanded by Lieutenant Colonel Michael S Currin went the first eight miles by water, and then headed into the jungle. It took them four days of hard and continuous

Left: *An "alligator" hits the beach and troops disembark during training.*
Below: *Marines race from their landing boats into the jungle on Bougainville, November 1943.*

trekking before they came out and hit the unsuspecting Japanese garrisons on both sides of the Viru. Since only eight Marines were killed during the action, luck had been on the side of the Raiders. Meanwhile, Army troops and the 9th Marine Defense Battalion had landed on Rendova Island, directly across from Munda Point. The Japanese sent up every available aircraft they had but the Americans were more than a match for them. The final tally was 101 enemy planes shot down. On 5 July the Army crossed over to Zanana Beach on New Georgia. Colonel Harry Liversedge took the 1st Raider Battalion of Lieutenant Colonel Griffiths, and two battalions of the 37th Infantry Division ashore to set up a blocking force behind Munda Point at Rice Anchorage. Liversedge advanced with his 2600 men toward Bairoko Harbor to insure that Munda's defenders did not escape. In the next three days of heavy fighting the soldiers and Marines fought side by side, and on occasions shared the same wet poncho. The Raiders kept up the pressure on the Japanese until although out of food for over 24 hours, they succeeded in driving the enemy out of the village of Enogai. The Raiders immediately

seized the 140mm coastal guns and later, on 10 July, an Army unit brought up rations for the starving Marines. On 18 July Currin's 4th Raider Battalion arrived to boost Liversedge's force. The next objective was Bairoko Harbor close to Munda. Liversedge set out on 20 July along the coast with the Marines, and dispatched the soldiers across the Dragon's Peninsula. From the very beginning nothing went right for Liversedge's Marines; the air strike that he had requested earlier never came. Intelligence once again had let them down. The Marines ran into

Above: *Marines move through the mud-swamped jungle to reach the front line on Bougainville.*

Japanese hidden machine-gun positions and snipers with Nambu guns superbly camouflaged in trees. The Marines fought a tremendously hard battle for seven straight hours, attacking, fighting off counterattacks, making flanking maneuvers, throwing in their last reserves, and looking for an army battalion which never got there in time. The Marines were forced to stop only 300 yards from their objective. With

Left: *Two Marines on a patrol engage in mopping up operations on Cape Torokina, Bougainville.*

over 200 wounded Raiders, Liversedge ordered his men back to Enogai. The 25th Infantry Division entered Bairoko soon afterwards and found it abandoned. The Raider battalions were decimated and only half of their remaining strength was fit for further combat duty after the Bairoko fight. They were returned to Guadalcanal to recuperate. The entire operation was a shambles from the beginning. Munda finally fell to the US Army on 5 August but the cost hardly justified the ends.

The next phase in the Solomons was masterminded by Halsey, who leap-frogged heavily fortified Kolombangara Island, north of New Georgia, and instead assaulted the weakly defended island of Vella Lavella. American air power was increasing in strength throughout the Pacific and continued to hammer Rabaul. The Marine "pilot of the moment" was Major Gregory "Pappy" Boyington. His squadron was VMF-214, the "Black Sheep Squadron." His first month with VMF-214 saw them knock down 57 Japanese aircraft. Boyington later earned the Medal of Honor and became the Marine Corps' highest ranking ace with 28 kills to his credit. However all good things come to an end, and on 3 January 1944, he was forced to parachute to safety and was picked up by a Japanese submarine. He was subsequently imprisoned for the duration of the war.

In the fall of 1943 three Marine divisions were in the Pacific Theater:

1st Division – to assault Cape Gloucester, New Britain
2nd Division – to assault Tarawa, in the Gilberts
3rd Division – to assault Bougainville

Bougainville would give the Allies the valuable airfield required to bring them within land-based fighter range of Rabaul. The planners decided to send the 8th New Zealand Brigade Group against the Treasury Islands as a diversionary move. The other feint was led by Lieutenant Colonel Victor Krulak, and 656 Marines of the 2nd Parachute Battalion against the Japanese-held island of Choiseul. Krulak had to make his attack look like a major landing. After hitting the beach at Choiseul, the 2nd Paras headed for

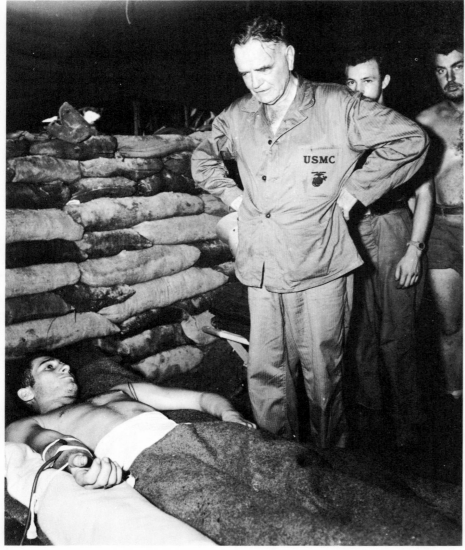

Left: *Vice-Admiral William Halsey visits a sandbagged hospital dugout on a beach-head at Bougainville. The patient, Private 1st Class Caruso, was recovering from an appendectomy.*

Above: *A dead Japanese on Bougainville.*
Right: *Attracted by the noise of gun fire, two Marines rush forward. A tank patrol had been ambushed by well-camouflaged Japanese.*

Sagigai the enemy's major barge base. The Marines hit Sagigai from both flanks. In an hour long hand-to-hand fight, the Japanese were decimated for a Marine loss of four killed and 12 wounded in action. Krulak himself was wounded in the fight but recovered. By the next night his men were withdrawn from Choiseul and the main Bougainville landings were in the mill.

The main landing site was only 210 miles from Rabaul. The island itself was an even less inviting location than Guadalcanal. There were an estimated 17,000 Japanese troops at the southern end of the island; an additional 5000 at the far northern tip, but only a meager 300 at Cape Torokina where the actual landings were going to be made. On 1 November 1943 the 3rd Marine Division began landing at Bougainville. The 3rd Marines were commanded by Major General Allen Turnage and composed of the 3rd, 9th and 21st Marines, with the artillery of the 12th Marines, an engineers outfit from the 19th Marines and a detachment of Seabees. The Marines suffered heavy losses getting ashore but once on the beaches they dug in and consolidated their positions. The Marines knocked out all 25 of Cape Torokina's protective bunker emplacements. The Japanese hit the Marines with everything they had from machine guns to 75mm guns but to no avail. By that evening 14,000 Marines were ashore. That night, the Navy fought the Battle of Empress Augusta Bay. Task Force 29 destroyed a Japanese cruiser and destroyer, but more important protected the beach-head. Meanwhile, the Marines were getting on with their job of extending their perimeter and building an airfield. Although the enemy was about to surrender, it tried to drive the Marines out by landing a counter force of 475 troops on their northern flank. This attack was dealt with speedily by the Marine defenders and by the next day the Japanese force had been eliminated. A site for the airfield was selected 1500 yards inland from the Marine positions, and the 2nd Battalion, 21st Marines were sent to secure the area. The only problem was that the enemy got there first.

The subsequent fight was named the Battle of Piva Forks. It began on 24 November, Thanksgiving Day, when two battalions of the 3rd Marines crossed the east branch of the Piva River. The 3rd Battalion on the left had to fight another hand-to-hand engagement before routing the enemy. By the time the Marines had reached their specific objectives, they had sustained 115 casualties and killed in the vicinity of 1071 enemy soldiers. Back on the

Below: *The US Marines used dogs for scouting and running messages in the jungles of Bougainville.*

beach, a consignment of turkeys had been brought ashore compliments of the US Navy. The cooks did not waste any time but started roasting them as fast as they could and sending them forward to the men on the line. The Marines continued to fight until by the end of January 1944, they were withdrawn. The total price for this adventure was 423 killed and 1418 wounded in action on Bougainville. The airfield was ready; and now bombing missions could be escorted all the way into Rabaul by land-based fighters. American air power began to bomb Rabaul intensively until the remaining Japanese air strength was withdrawn to Truk. Rabaul was to become but a name in history – the one-time great Japanese strategic base was now impotent thanks to the joint efforts of the US Marines and their Air Force counterparts.

While the 3rd Marine Division secured Bougainville, MacArthur had committed the 1st Marine Division to take Cape Gloucester in New Britain because he did not want the Japanese on his flank as he moved up the coast toward New Guinea. The 1st Marine Division assaulted Cape Gloucester on 26 December 1943. They were commanded by Major General Rupertus, an excellent leader. The first units ashore were Colonel Julian Frisbie's 1st and 3rd Battalions, the 7th Marines which landed just east of the cape. The next units in were the 3rd Battalion, 1st Marines. On the opposite side of the cape, Lieutenant Colonel James Masters' 2nd Battalion, 1st Marines landed near Tauali and proceeded to set up a trail block in the jungle. The landings went smoothly and by nightfall 11,000 men were ashore. The 1st Marine Division then waited for the Japanese night attack, and when it came they fought all night long. This continuous fighting went on for the next few days but surprisingly enough got weaker and weaker. The 1st Marines commanded by Colonel William Whaling advanced on the cape's airfield. Tanks and flamethrowers had to be utilized to drive the Japanese out of their fortified positions around the airfield. By 29 December the airfield was in the hands of the Marines. The Japanese made one last-ditch fight on Razorback Hill, south of the airfield, but Lieutenant Colonel Lewis Walt's 2nd Battalion, 5th Marines proved to be too much for the enemy who were virtually destroyed to a man. On 31 December 1943 Major General Rupertus raised the American flag over Cape Gloucester. MacArthur, first to send congratulations, said: "Your gallant division has maintained the immortal record of the Marine Corps and covered itself with glory."

Left: *These men fell back to the beaches when Japanese boats appeared off shore. They returned to their positions once they had driven the boats away.*

Two days later, the 3rd Battalion, 7th Marines moved south through typical damp jungle toward Borgen Bay. The Marines came to a greenish jungle stream which was about 20 feet wide and were stopped cold. Every time a Marine tried to cross over he was picked off by snipers on the other side. The jungle foliage was so thick and impenetrable that they could not even discern the source of the enemy gunfire. The Japanese, as always clever jungle fighters, had dug in behind log emplacements and foxholes well concealed by the undergrowth. The Marines named the stream "Suicide Creek." They attempted to flank the Japanese positions but still could not eliminate them. Numerous attempts were made but all met with negative results. Finally General Rupertus and Lt Colonel "Chesty" Puller, executive officer, 7th Marines determined to get the 3rd Battalion on the move. Marine engineers were called in and proceeded to demolish the 12-foot high bank on Suicide Creek; a temporary road was speedily built across the swamp wide enough for Sherman tanks to give close support to the "Mud Marines." The Marines then moved across the creek and after some extremely tough fight-

ing eradicated the Japanese. The result of this action was 41 killed and 218 wounded in action.

The Marines had one more objective, Aogiri Ridge where the remainder of the main Japanese force was entrenched. By the time Walt's and Puller's men had taken the ridge on 11 January, the attackers were in need of a rest, especially after going through five bayonet charges by the Japanese. On 16 January the last enemy counterattack was beaten and the Cape Gloucester campaign completed. This brief campaign had cost the US Marines 310 killed and 1083 wounded in action. The 1st Marine Division was getting ready to leave New Britain and in need of a much deserved rest but the noose around Rabaul was tightened by the time they left. In April 1944 Marine ground forces in the Pacific were returned to the operational control of Admiral Nimtz in the Central Pacific. But the Marine air units were assigned to MacArthur in the Southwest Pacific, the Marines would not join up with their own close air support units until the Okinawa campaign. The New Britain campaign was finished but the next pin was already on the map – it pointed to Tarawa.

Below: *Corporals Mancinger and Holly relax in their camp.*
Below left: *Despite heavy casualties the Marines held their ground.*

Gilberts

Tarawa was a small triangular atoll, 12 miles wide and 18 miles long. On the tiny island of Betio, at the southwest tip of the atoll was a small airfield. Betio was three miles long and only 600 yards wide. The Japanese had learned their lesson at Makin and made this small island into a first-class fortress. There were 200 guns around the perimeter, manned by 2600 well-trained Imperial troops and 2000 civilian laborers. The Japanese thought that Betio was impregnable and that no American force would be able to crack its defenses. The actual assault on Tarawa was the beginning of the island-hopping route to Japan through the Central Pacific. The 2nd Marine Division (nicknamed the "Bloody Second") was to take Tarawa. The V Amphibious Corps Reconnaissance Company was to occupy Apamama, south of Tarawa. The 167th Regimental Combat Team, 27th Infantry Division was to take Makin.

Prior to the landings, the navy shelled Tarawa and Betio with the greatest naval barrage ever used against such a small target. The landing started with three waves. On Red Beach 3, Major Crowe's 3rd Battalion, 8th Marines hit the beach at 0910 hours. On Red Beach 1, on the west, Major John Schoettel's 3rd Battalion, 2nd Marines landed at 0917 hours despite extremely heavy casualties. At 0959 hours Schoettel notified command that the issue was in grave doubt. He was ordered to commit his reserve; he screamed into the radio, "We have nothing left to land." The extremely narrow beaches were backed by a coconut log seawall four feet high. Fifteen feet behind the wall, Rear Admiral Keiji Shibasaki had placed machine-gun nests and artillery emplacements to destroy any attempt to climb over the seawall. It was because of this that the first three waves of Marines were still pinned to the beachheads. Colonel David Shoup was the assault commander. He had the naval support ships bombard the eastern end of the island. He sent Major Wood Kyle's 1st Battalion, 2nd Marines to the center beach, with orders to move westward and help the troops on Red 1. He dispatched half of Major Robert Ruud's 3rd Battalion, 8th Marines to back up Crowe on Red 3. Ruud's men advanced as ordered, under heavy fire and in deep water for over 700 yards; some drowned, others were shot. Of Ruud's entire first wave, only 100 made it ashore. The second wave took shelter near the pier, and still the casualties were mounting. The entire third wave was all but slaughtered. A few men of the fourth wave managed to land; the rest could not make it. It was 1200 hours, the attack was stalled, and some 5000 Marines were trapped on the beaches on the edge of Betio; 1500 had been killed or wounded.

Major General Julian Smith, 2nd Division commander, radioed Major General Holland Smith, V Marine Amphibious Corps, who was on Rear Admiral Turner's flagship off Makin. He asked for the corps reserve, the 6th

Right: *The first casualties at Tarawa, where the Marines learned a bitter lesson.*
Below: *The amphibious tractors used in the Tarawa landings could climb over the coral reefs, but many did not make it to the beaches.*

Above: *The survivors of the landings fought with such determination that they drove the Japanese inland.*
Above left: *Marines picked off the Japanese on the Betio airport one by one, as they made suicidal counterattacks.*
Above far left: *Marines carry a wounded buddy back to a landing barge.*
Left: *Having finally wiped out a garrison of over 3000, Marines withdraw from Tarawa to take a well-earned rest.*

Marines, who were being held off Tarawa to support either invasion if required. Turner granted this request, and Jules Smith then committed his own reserve the 1st Battalion, 8th Marines. Communications broke down and these men were still waiting in their boats past midnight. The Marines waited all night for the dreaded Japanese night attack but it never materialized. There was a stench of dead which pervaded the entire stretch of beach on Betio. The next day at dawn, Shoup ordered the Marines to break out, everywhere small groups of Marines advanced slowly, throwing grenades and blocks of TNT into bunkers and pillboxes. By 1200 hours the advance was picking up momentum and for the first time the Marines felt as if victory was just possible.

Heavy fighting continued throughout the day. Finally on D-Day plus three, Betio was secured, the Marines were reopening the airstrip and the last pockets of resistance were being cleaned up. Of a total of 4836 Japanese soldiers and Korean civilian laborers on Betio, only 146 were captured, 4690 were killed. Marine and Naval losses were 1113 killed in action, and 2290 wounded in action, an enormous number of men for so small an island,

and one which could have been by-passed. In Major General Holland Smith's own words:

Was Tarawa worth it? My answer is unqualified: No. From the very beginning the decision of the Joint Chiefs to seize Tarawa was a mistake and from their initial mistake grew the terrible drama of errors, errors of omission rather than commission, resulting in these needless casualties. . . . Tarawa should have been by-passed. Its capture – a mission executed by Marines under direct orders from the high command – was a terrible waste of life and effort. . . . The futile sacrifice of Marines on that strategically useless coral strand makes me sad today as it did then. . . . In the strategical scheme of the Central Pacific offensive, it taught me that the instrument of high policy known as the Joint Chiefs of Staff was not infallible. Tarawa was a mistake.

The Marshalls and Marianas

The US and her Allies were on the offensive and Japan was being slowly driven back. The primary question now facing the Allied planners was exactly how was Japan ultimately to be defeated. Germany was still the main Allied objective and Japan was secondary, but the invasion of Normandy was in the final stages and everything was going according to plan. After much interservice bickering, and in spite of MacArthur's objections, the US Navy's overall strategy for ending the Pacific war had the support of the

Left: *Major General Holland Smith and his staff observe the bombing of Kwajalein, prior to the landing.*
Right: *Crew of an LST prepare to launch the LVTs destined for Roi Island.*

January 1944. The primary attack was to be against Kwajalein atoll, the key to the Japanese outer defensive perimeter and the center of Japanese air power in the islands. Majuro was to be taken first and utilized as an anchorage for the fleet and mobile service squadron. Eniwetok, 330 miles away, was of secondary importance and was to be occupied after Kwajalein. The other four major atolls were to be by-passed and neutralized by the fast carrier force and land-based aircraft.

Kwajalein is the largest true atoll in the world. The two points selected for seizure were the twin islands of Roi-Namur, where the airfield was located, and Kwajalein Island, the main naval base and distribution center in the chain. During the morning of 1 February 1944 the 4th Marine Division went ashore on the lagoon side of Roi-Namur and by 2 February all resistance had ceased. Kwajalein Island fell to the Army's 32nd and 184th Regiments of the 7th Division in

USAAF. The XX and XXI Bomber Commands wanted bases from which to launch their B-29 Superfortresses against the Japanese homeland. They envisaged and rightly so, that the war could be won from the air. If the Army Air Force could bomb Japan into submission all the better, because if mainland Japan had to be invaded, American casualties, it was estimated, would reach the one million mark. To capture the necessary airfields for the Air Force, Nimitz secured with un-

expected ease his first main objective, the Marshall Islands.

The Marshall Islands have the same physical characteristics as the Gilberts. They are made up of hundreds of coral atolls and islands covering 400,000 square miles of ocean. They are in two parallel chains roughly 100 miles apart. In the northeast are the large atolls of Majuro, Maloelap, Mille and Wotje. The southern chain consists of Eniwetok, Jaluit and Kwajalein. The assault on the Marshalls was set for 31

Above: *Brigadier General Erskine, Major Generals Schmidt and Holland Smith discuss future operations.*

a four-day fight. The quick victory at Kwajalein took the high command by surprise. The 4th Marine Division had lost 313 killed and 502 wounded in action, and inflicted 3563 casualties on the enemy.

The next phase went straight ahead; on the night of 12/13 February, three of the fast carrier groups under Spruance hit Truk. The results were spectacular: 20,000 tons of shipping sunk or severely damaged. Japanese naval losses were 270 aircraft, two light cruisers, four destroyers and numerous support ships. Now the assault on Eniwetok could begin without any interference. Eniwetok was another

Below: *The amphtracks head for Namur and Roi on the day after the main landings had been successfully accomplished.*

Left: *A wounded Marine gets an emergency blood transfusion on the beach at Namur. The 4th Marine Division overran the Japanese positions after 24 hours' fighting.*

Above: *The commanding officers and visiting dignitaries inspect the battlefield at Namur, left to right: Admiral Spruance; unknown; James Forrestal, Secretary of the Navy; Major General Schmidt; Major General Holland Smith; Admiral Connolly; Colonel Evans Carlson; Admiral Pownall.*

substantial atoll. It was made up of three main islands: Engebi, in the north which had an airfield, and Eniwetok and Parry in the south. On the night of 18 February the Navy bombarded Parry and Eniwetok Islands, in preparation for the morning amphibious landings. Two battalions of the 106th Infantry took Eniwetok on the 19th and the island was completely secure by the 21st. The following day the Marines took Parry Island after three days of heavy bombardment.

Meanwhile, on 18 February the 22nd Marines, commanded by Colonel John Walker, attacked Engebi. The fighting was fierce and the 1200 Japanese defenders gave everything they had in the defense of the tiny island but to no avail. By 1500 hours Engebi was secure, 1000 enemy were dead and the 22nd Marines had lost 64 killed, 81 missing and 158 wounded in action. The Marine and Army units had taken the Marshalls three months ahead of time. The captured Japanese airfields and bases were quickly repaired and gave the Allies facilities 2500 miles closer to Japan than Pearl Harbor. With the fall of the Marshalls, Nimitz put forward his plans to assault the Japanese-held Mariana Islands.

The Central Pacific saw a brief respite after the fall of the Marshall Islands. Preparations were underway for a major offensive against the Marianas. The Marianas form a vital link in an almost unbroken chain of islands running 1500 miles southward from Tokyo. The group is composed of some 15 islands, but only the four largest were of military value: Saipan, Rota, Tinian and Guam. Saipan was

Right: *Mopping up in the Marshalls: Marines wade ashore in April 1944, only to find that the Japanese had evacuated Aur Island long before.*

only 1200 miles from Tokyo and this made it closer to Japan than any other mandated island. With its neighboring island of Tinian, it was the key to the Marianas' defense. Saipan had two airfields and a seaplane base; Tinian had two airfields. Together they served as the main refueling points on the air ferry route between Japan and the south. Guam had two additional airfields and a third under construction was capable of taking the largest bombers known. The Japanese were not willing to let these necessary and vital islands go without a stiff fight. The garrison on Saipan was 32,000 strong, on Tinian 9000 strong and in Guam 18,000 strong. The US invasion of the Marianas called for the seizure of Saipan, Tinian and Guam. D-Day for Saipan was scheduled for 15 June 1944. The island is 14 miles long and 6.5 miles wide, encompassing about 72 square miles. In the center of the island is Mount Tapotchau which is 1500 feet high. The Japanese had completed an airfield at Aslito in the south and were constructing another in the north. In addition, an airstrip was being built on the west side of the island near the town of Charan Kanoa. The plan was to land on the southern portion of the west coast, advance rapidly and seize the high ground. The 2nd Marine Division was ordered to seize Mount Tapotchau; the 4th Marine Division was to take Aslito airfield and move across the island to the east coast. This operation was the largest to date in the Pacific, involving over 500 vessels, carrying four and a half assault divisions. The logistic difficulties were tremendous.

On 15 June 1944 the 2nd and 4th Marine Divisions began landing on

Above: *Clearing Saipan, Marines blow up a Japanese dugout position.*
Below: *The first landings on Saipan on the morning of 15 June 1944.*

Above: *The first Marines ashore dig into position on Saipan. Note the smoke in the background from a burning amphtrack.*
Left: *Moving forward cautiously these Marines take cover in a shell hole.*

Saipan after an intense pre-landing bombardment by the US Naval Bombardment Group. The Japanese were driven from their beach fortifications by the naval gunfire and took to the high positions inland. From there they launched a heavy attack against the landing forces backed up by artillery and mortar fire. By sunset 20,000 Marines were ashore and a beach-head established 1500 yards in depth. Spruance received news that evening that the Japanese fleet had passed through the San Bernardino Straits and was proceeding toward the Marianas. Realizing that the enemy was seeking a fleet action, Spruance called a halt to the projected landings on Guam and ordered the 27th Infantry Division, the reserve, to be landed on Saipan. He withdrew all transports to the east where they would be safe.

The 2nd Division suffered heavy casualties on Saipan. The Japanese defenders knew that they had to win

Right: *Leathernecks use a Japanese mountain gun to shell positions in Garapan, the capital city of Saipan.*

Right: *Leathernecks use a Japanese mountain gun to shell positions in Garapan, the capital city of Saipan.*

otherwise the US would mount air attacks on Tokyo. There were 78,000 men ashore when the US Navy left Saipan and headed for the largest carrier action of the time. The fast carrier groups of Mitscher's Task Force 58, totally destroyed the enemy aircraft on Guam. The Japanese then launched four gigantic air attacks against the US fleet in the Marianas. In the following two days the American pilots shot down 476 enemy planes in what became known as "the Great Marianas Turkey Shoot." The Battle of the Philippine Sea as the naval fight was known, did not destroy the Japanese surface fleet. It did, however, give the US complete control of the air and sea and led to the speedy conclusion of the Marianas campaign. The Japanese on Saipan, now in a hopeless situation, continued to fight on. Major General Holland Smith turned his full attention to destroying the Japanese garrison. The 6th Marines had taken Mount Tipo Pale and the 8th Marines were busy assaulting Mount Tapotchau. Meanwhile, Holland Smith and Major General Ralph Smith, 27th Infantry Division commander, got into a controversy which was later to extend all the way to Chief of Staff, General George Marshall. Ralph Smith contravened an order of his superior, Holland Smith, and the Marine general relieved him of his duty and replaced him with Major General Sanderford Jarman. The top Army officer in the Central Pacific, Lieutenant General Robert Richardson, convened a board of inquiry to investigate what was considered a direct affront to the Army. Lieutenant General Simon Buckner, as the chairman of the board, found that Holland Smith had over-reacted, but was within his right to remove Ralph Smith. Holland Smith was placed in charge of the Fleet Marine Force, Pacific, which had no control over Army units; and Ralph Smith was transferred to Europe.

The entire campaign of Saipan took three and a half weeks and at 1615 hours on 9 July, Vice-Admiral Turner stated that Saipan was secure. The cost of Saipan was 3426 Americans killed and 13,099 wounded in action. Japanese dead were estimated to be over 38,500.

Tinian was the next stop, just three miles across the channel to the south. It had two superb airfields: one at Ushi Point consisting of two airstrips, and

Right: *The 37 mm gun could knock out the smaller Japanese tanks but was useless against tanks in Europe.*

Division had lost 105 men killed and 653 wounded in action and the 4th Marine Division lost 212 killed and 897 wounded in action. The Japanese lost over 5000 troops in the battle.

The final stage in the Marianas campaign was the recapture of Guam. There were twice as many Japanese troops on Guam as on Tinian, and because of the one month delay in the actual assault, the Japanese had more than enough time to prepare a real welcome for the Marines. In the 21 days that it took to recapture Guam US losses were 1744 killed and 6540 wounded in action. In Guam hundreds

Left: Marines take up position behind an abandoned enemy truck as they try to flush out snipers in Garapan.
Below: Japanese ships in Tanapag Harbor tried to evacuate some of the Saipan garrison. Marine artillery cut short their escape.

one at Gurgan Point on the western side of the island. The Japanese were constructing a third field near Tinian Town on the southwest coast. After Smith took over as Fleet Marine commander, Major General Harry Schmidt assumed command of V Amphibious Corps and Major General Clifton Cates replaced Schmidt as 4th Division commander.

At 0747 hours on 24 July E Company, 24th Marines landed on White Beach 1. The Marines wiped out the small defending beach force and moved inland to make room for the remainder of the 2nd Battalion. In less than an hour, the 1st and 2nd Battalions, 24th Marines were ashore. White Beach 2 was a different proposition. The Marines had to avoid the

Below: As the Marines mop up on Saipan, a flame-throwing tank smothers a Japanese pillbox.

beach area until the mines could be cleared away which meant that they had to climb up the nearby rocky ledges. By 0930 hours, the 25th Marines had established a beach-head 1500 yards deep and 4000 wide. Major General Cates brought ashore his reserves, the 23rd Marines, to bolster the beach defenses, as he believed that the Japanese would launch a night counterattack. He was right and that night proved to be one of the hardest fought night engagements that the Marines had fought. On 25 July the 8th Marines landed and in co-ordination with the 24th Marines occupied a portion of Ushi Field. The 25th Marines took 290-foot Mount Maga while the 23rd Marines continued to push south. By 26 July the 8th Marines controlled all of Ushi Field. Major General Schmidt declared the island secured by 1900 hours on 1 August. In conquering Tinian the 2nd Marine

of Japanese soldiers held out in the numerous mountain caves and in the rocky coastal caves for over three months. It took an entire Marine regiment that long to mop up. With the capture of Guam and Tinian the campaign for the Marianas was complete.

Peleliu

In August 1944 strategy in the Pacific was still governed by the Joint Chiefs of Staff directive of 12 March. After the capture of the Marianas, the Central Pacific Forces, commanded by Admiral Nimitz, were to occupy the Palau Islands. These islands were 500 miles out in the middle of nowhere. Admiral William Halsey was against the entire operation in the Palaus. He believed and rightly so, that the entire scheme was unnecessary. This chain should

have been by-passed, but was not because Nimitz had to protect Mac-Arthur's move into the Philippines. Consequently Nimitz ordered the Marines to take Peleliu. This island strongpoint was the scene of a new Japanese defensive tactic. No longer would they defend the beaches and take great losses fighting over fixed positions. Instead of trying to drive the Marines off the beaches, the Japanese dug into caves in the Umurbrogol ridges in the center of the island so that the Marines would have to fight from cave to cave in a time-consuming operation which would be costly both in men and equipment.

Peleliu was only six miles long and two miles wide; but its garrison was composed of 10,200 highly trained Japanese troops. The Japanese had mined the beaches, put underwater obstacles on the approaches to the beaches and dug anti-tank trenches; all

of these were linked by a specially worked-out crossfire which would decimate any force attempting to get through. They were prepared to fight to the bitter end and that is exactly what they did. On the morning of 15 September 1944 the 1st Marine Division assaulted Peleliu. Colonel Chesty Puller's 1st Marines assaulted the Umurbrogol ridges slightly north of Peleliu's airfield. Colonel Bucky Harris' 5th Marines plunged straight across the island to take the airfield. Colonel Haiti Hanneken's 7th Marines moved on the right flank to secure the southern portion of the island. The Marines had only one reserve battalion, the 2nd of the 7th Marines, which was in no way prepared for battle. The odds were definitely against the Marines, 9000 Leathernecks against 10,000 dug-in enemy troops. Puller did not like the look of the operation, but Major General Rupertus,

1st Division commander, did not want any Army troops on Peleliu if he could help it. In the first three days of fighting, the Marines advanced through artillery fire and withstood a massive enemy counterattack. Water became critical; there just was not enough to go round. To make matters worse, the Marines were having to utilize flamethrowers to get the Japanese out of their caves and fortified ridge positions. D-Day plus three days and the Marines had lost 47 men killed and 414 wounded in action, and killed 2600 of the enemy. The heat was tremendous – over 110 degrees. Men were dropping like flies. Casualties were exceedingly high. One month after the initial landing, there were still over 1150 Japanese troops still holding out. The island was secure except for the small pocket holding the remaining Japanese troops. The 1st Marine Division sustained 1124 men killed, 117 missing and an unbelievable 5024 wounded in action. The Japanese final death count was 10,200, practically the whole defense force.

Above: *The hill on Peleliu where this incident occurred was renamed Suicide.*
Below: *Landing craft scurry forward to the beaches of Peleliu.*

The 1st Marine Division headed back to Pavuvu for a much-deserved rest. They never wanted to hear the name Peleliu again – it brought back bad memories. The Marines assaulted Peleliu in direct support of MacArthur's Philippine invasion, yet they did not take an active part in that operation. The only Marines to fight in the Philippines were Brigadier General Thomas Bourke's Artillery Command of the V Amphibious Corps totalling some 1500 men and the aviators of the 1st MAW. Even this involvement was an accident; during the Marianas campaign, the artillerymen had exchanged places with their Army counterparts and the mix-up was never sorted out. The Marine gunners landed north of Dulag on Leyte, on the 23 October 1944 and were in support of the Army advance. The Marine artillerymen were finally pulled out of the Leyte offensive on 13 December. Meanwhile the Marine aviators were getting ready to fight a new threat, the Japanese kamikaze pilot. Also they had been too involved in shooting down enemy aircraft and their main mission had been forgotten – the support of Marine ground units. The entire Marine Aviation program was reorganized so that they received their own escort carriers. They were organized into a truly tactical command and were better for it. With MacArthur's reconquest of the Philippines, the stage was again set for another advance. The next stop in the Pacific War was going to be Iwo Jima.

Iwo Jima

Iwo Jima is an island in the Bonin chain and is only four and a half miles long, and two and a quarter miles wide. It is nestled at the southern end of the chain which extends due south for 700 miles from the coast of Japan. The entire island is flat except for the rocky promontory of Mount Suribachi, an extinct volcano, which is 556 feet high on the southern portion of the island. Iwo Jima was of great importance to the Japanese who used it for staging purposes on their routes to the central and southern Pacific. The early years of the war saw them build two airfields on it and after the fall of the Marshall Islands their importance grew. The conquest of the Marianas by the United States in July 1944 and its subsequent utilization for air attacks against the homeland, even further enhanced the importance of Iwo Jima. It was more than evident that the Americans would need it for a staging point and advanced air base for the ultimate invasion of Japan. The Japanese realized this and in early 1944 dispatched the 109th Division to the island. This unit was commanded by Lieutenant General Kuribayashi. He immediately strengthened all defenses, and began work on a third airfield in the north. Kuribayashi knew that the beaches could not be held and so he based his entire defensive strategy on a do-or-die effort around Mount Suribachi and the Motoyama plateau. The US constantly bombarded the island but nonetheless, defensive positions

were built in-depth between No 1 and No 2 airfields, and between No 2 airfield and Motoyama, connected by a very intricate network of tunnels. These defenses were supported by heavy artillery and mortars conveniently situated in caves and camouflaged concrete emplacements. The same type of defenses were built around Mount Suribachi and, in addition, the beaches were heavily mined. By January 1945 the Iwo Jima garrison was over 21,000 strong.

Admiral Nimitz placed the entire operation in the capable hands of Admiral Raymond Spruance and his 5th Fleet. The man in charge of the

Above left: *Lieutenant Wade assesses the overall importance of target at a pre-invasion briefing of the 4th Marine Division.*
Below: *The Leathernecks found it tough establishing a toehold on the beaches of Iwo Jima.*

actual Joint Expeditionary Force was Vice-Admiral Kelly Turner and the 5th US Marine Amphibious Corps, consisting of the 3rd, 4th and 5th Marine Divisions, were given the task of seizing the island. Rear Admiral Marc Mitscher's fast carrier force was given the covering task. Spruance knew all about the heavy Japanese preparations so he arranged for the 7th USAAF to attack the island's defenses with B-24s from the Marianas. This continuous bombardment was to start on 31 January and continue until 15 February. Then a three-day naval bombardment was to begin. To create a diversion to pull away any Japanese air support for the island, Spruance ordered the fast carrier force to attack targets in the Tokyo area for the first time on 16 and 17 February.

The Amphibious Support Force arrived off Iwo Jima on 16 February and proceeded to soften the Japanese defenses. At precisely 0600 hours on 19

Above: *On 19 February the 4th Marine Division took part in its fourth amphibious assault in thirteen months.*

Above: *Marines of the 5th Marine Division relax following the victory on Iwo Jima.*
Below: *A flame thrower of E Company prepares to assault a Japanese pillbox on Airfield No 2.*

February 1945 Turner arrived with the main force. Directly after dawn the most concentrated pre-landing bombardment of the war was initiated by seven battleships, seven cruisers and numerous destroyers against shore defenses. During this bombardment over 31,000 shells were fired and in addition the fast carrier force strafed the beaches, known defensive positions and camouflaged artillery for over 25 minutes. The first Marines were landing on the southeastern beaches by 0900 hours. Although the naval and air bombardments were tremendous, the damage to defensive works was minimal. Once the initial landings were accomplished the Japanese garrison erupted from their hidden caves and underground shelters, and the Marines were immediately pinned down on the beaches. The weather, always a factor in amphibious landings, changed for the worse. Rising surf and extremely

strong currents delayed landing reinforcements, tanks and stores of equipment. The Marines were hard pressed but undaunted – as usual they plowed ahead.

One specific action earned Sergeant Darrell Cole the Medal of Honor for conspicuous gallantry above and beyond the call of duty. While acting as leader of a machine gun section of B Company, First Battalion, 23rd Marines, 4th Marine Division, Sergeant Cole was advancing with one squad of his section in the initial assault wave under heavy small arms, mortar and artillery fire, up the sloping beach toward No 1 airfield when he personally, at an extremely high risk to himself, destroyed two hostile emplacements which were endangering his unit's progress with hand grenades. Continuing to advance they were brought under tremendous enemy fire which succeeded in bringing their

Top: *An observer pinpoints a machine-gun nest on his map so that an artillery unit can eliminate it.*
Above: *Members of the 5th Marines display their spoils of war, which were taken in the first days of fighting.*

Above: *Marines engage in direct frontal assaults on Japanese positions in Iwo.*

advance to a halt. Sergeant Cole set up one of his machine guns and managed to eliminate one of the enemy pillboxes. He quickly made an on-the-spot tactical judgment and armed only with a

Below: *Raising the flag on Mount Suribachi: most of these Marines were later killed in action.*

pistol and one hand grenade, advanced alone against the remaining two enemy pillboxes. He threw his hand grenade into the enemy pillbox, and returned for another grenade. He ran withering machine-gun fire from the enemy not once but three times before he succeeded in destroying all of the enemy positions. For this superb action under constant enemy fire, he was awarded the highest honor that a grateful country can bestow upon a

Medal of honor winners – Iwo Jima campaign 1945

Name	Unit
Corporal Charles Berry	26th Marines
Private William Caddy	26th Marines
Lieutenant-Colonel Justice Chambers	25th Marines
Sergeant Darrell Cole	23rd Marines
Captain Robert Dunlap	26th Marines
Sergeant Ross Gray	25th Marines
Sergeant William Harrell	28th Marines
Private Douglas Jacobson	23rd Marines
Sergeant Joseph Julian	27th Marines
Private James LaBelle	27th Marines
2nd Lieutenant John Leims	9th Marines
Private Jacklyn Lucas	26th Marines
1st Lieutenant Jack Lummus	27th Marines
1st Lieutenant Harry Martin	5th Pioneer Battalion
Captain Joseph McCarthy	24th Marines
Private George Phillips	28th Marines
Private Donald Ruhl	28th Marines
Private Franklin Sigler	26th Marines
Corporal Tony Stein	28th Marines
Gunnery Sergeant William Walsh	27th Marines
Private Wilson Watson	9th Marines
Corporal Hershel Williams	21st Marines

Total: 22

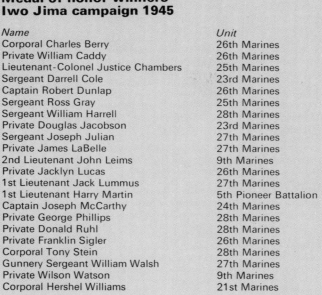

hero. This was only one of 22 Medal-of-Honor winners at Iwo Jima.

By the evening of 19 February the Marines had secured a beach-head only 1000 yards deep at the edge of No 1 airfield, and reached the west coast at the foot of Mount Suribachi. In the next ten days the Marines slowly overcame the stubborn and gallant Japanese defenses. On 23 February 1945 Mount Suribachi was taken, No 1 airfield secured and the edge of No 2 airfield in sight. The Marines were in complete control of the island by 26 March. The action was the most costly to date in the Pacific. Practically the entire 21,000-man garrison of Iwo Jima were dead, and only about 2000 prisoners taken. Marine casualties were 6800 dead and 19,200 wounded.

Spruance's 5th Fleet was not left unmarked during the battle. On the night of 20/21 February 20 Japanese aircraft hit Mitscher's fast carrier force without much damage but the next day, the *Saratoga* was hit by five kamikazes, causing substantial damage. Only two hours later, another five attacked her but only one succeeded in reaching the ship. This time the damage was so extensive that the grand old lady had to return to the West Coast for major repairs. On that same evening two more kamikazes attacked the escort carrier *Bismarck Sea* and within a couple of hours that ship went down. Reprisal raids against Japan were launched from the fast carrier force on 25 February but they were for the most part ineffective; immediately afterwards bad weather set in. Mitscher then withdrew to his base at Ulithi. He did manage to make one parting strike against Okinawa on his way back. By 6 March P-51 Mustangs of the 7th USAAF began to utilize the airfields on Iwo Jima, and by April they were escorting B-29s into Japan. The Marines once again brought the war to a swifter conclusion by their initiative and devotion to duty. The taking of Iwo Jima, especially the final assault on Mount Suribachi will live forever in the annals of the US Marine Corps. It is best summarized by the following:

The raising of that flag on Suribachi means a Marine Corps for the next 500 years.
James Forrestal: To Lieutenant General Holland Smith, as the Marines raised the Colors on Mount Suribachi, 23 February 1945.

Left: *Two Marines blast their way through the labyrinth of defenses on Iwo Jima. The Japanese had dug into caves and it took five weeks to gain control of the island and a further two months of mopping up.*

Okinawa

The next major offensive was the assault on the Ryukyu Islands chain, and in particular the main island of Okinawa, the largest in that chain. It is only 340 miles from Formosa and 900 miles from Leyte. The main importance of this island was its three airfields – Kadena, Naha and Yontan – and two airstrips – Yonabaru and Machinato, which were to be used for the final phase of the air war against Japan.

The assault on Okinawa was planned for 1 April 1945 by the 10th US Army, commanded by Lieutenant General Simon Bolivar Buckner, consisting of the III Amphibious Corps (1st, 2nd and 6th Marine Divisions) and XXIV Corps, with an additional division held in reserve. All of these units which were committed to the offensive were specially trained outfits and had taken part in similar operations throughout

the Pacific Theater. The Naval Assault Force was very similar to the one utilized against Iwo Jima. Spruance was again in charge of the entire operation; Vice-Admiral Marc Mitscher had the fast carrier force; Vice-Admiral Turner had the Joint Expeditionary Force; and Vice-Admiral Sir Bernard Rawlings commanded the British Pacific Fleet (this latter consisted of the battleships *King George V* and *Howe*, carriers *Indomitable*, *Victorious*, *Indefatigable* and *Illustrious*, the cruisers *Swiftsure*, *Black Prince*, *Argonaut*, *Euryalus* and *Gambia*, and 11 destroyers.) Including the 5th Fleet Logistic Support Group, the entire armada totalled 1440 ships of various types.

On 18 and 19 March the fast carrier force was to attack airfields in Kyushu and shipping in the Inland Sea as a preliminary "softening up" process. The XXI Bomber Command in the Marianas was ordered to attack selected targets and various airfields in

Above: *Members of the 6th Marines Division move toward the Ishikawa Isthmus.*
Below: *The 1st Marine Division sweeps across Okinawa.*

Above: *Marines used explosives to drive the Japanese out of their fortified caves.*
Above left: *Major General Lemuel, Commanding General of the 6th Marine Division, traces the progress of his division on a map.*

With the invasion fleet in the background, US transports unload supplies on the beaches at Okinawa.

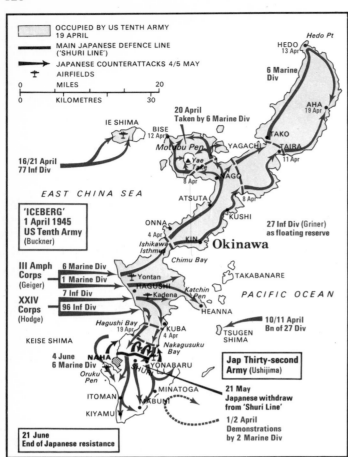

Kyushu between the 27–31 March, and in addition mine the Shimonoseki Strait through which the bulk of all Japanese shipping sailed. The Japanese ordered Lieutenant General Ushijima to defend the Ryukyus and hold them at all costs. His defense force consisted of the 24th, 28th and 62nd Divisions, and 44th Independent Mixed Brigade. The 9th Division was also to have been an integral part of the defense force but had been transferred to Formosa in December 1944 and had never been replaced. The actual location of the 28th Division was the Sakishima Islands, which left only two divisions and the one independent mixed brigade for the island garrison. Undaunted by the outlook which was anything but bright, Ushijima made two special infantry brigades, and one special regiment, totalling 13,500 men, from the air defense and other

Left: *Below the Shuri Castle, Marines found a snipers' nest in this church.*
Below left: *Marine Colonel Francis Fenton (kneeling) prays for his son Mike, only 19, who was killed during a Japanese counterattack.*
Below: *One Marine cries during the bitter fighting on the Shuri Line.*

administrative units on the island. He formed an Okinawa Home Guard unit consisting of 20,000 men to provide labor for construction tasks. His total strength, including a naval force of 10,000 men, came to 80,000 troops, which was quite a substantial garrison.

The preliminary moves were completed by the 31 March 1945 and D-Day was 1 April for the initial landings on Okinawa. Under a blistering naval bombardment, an unopposed amphibious landing was accomplished on the Hagushi beach. Opposition was slight, and by early evening both Yontan and Kadena airfields were secured. Everything was "looking good" and by 6 April the 10th Army held the center of the island and could now pivot in either direction. The Marine divisions had reached Nago at the base of the Motobu Peninsula, and both captured airfields were back in use. The first 72 hours of the invasion saw the Japanese 8th Air Division launch in excess of 80 aircraft to attack Allied shipping off Okinawa. The results were good: one destroyer, an escort carrier, two LST's, one LCT sunk, two transports badly damaged, and another six vessels receiving minor damage. The Japanese Combined Fleet commanded by Ad-

miral Toyoda ordered a naval force consisting of the battleship *Yamato* under Vice-Admiral Ito, the light cruiser *Yahagi* and eight destroyers to sail from the Inland Sea and engage Allied shipping off Okinawa on 8 April. This final act of bravado on the part of the Imperial Navy was very reminiscent of the sinking of the *Prince of Wales* and *Repulse* because they too lacked air cover. This force was sighted by a US submarine who relayed the important information to Mitscher. His aircraft located the enemy at 0822 hours on 7 April, 85 miles west of Kyushu. Two-hundred and ninety-six aircraft were in the air and poised for

Left: *Marine 1st Lieutenant David Douglas Duncan explains the operation of his camera to old Okinawan.*
Below: *Marines blast another cave.*
Right: *Two Marines armed with a Bazooka inch their way up a hill, two miles north of Naha.*

the attack at 1000 hours. Meanwhile, Turner had placed a strong force of battleships, cruisers and destroyers across the eventual path of the enemy force just in case it managed to elude or survive the massive air attack which was in process. By 1430 hours the power of the Imperial Navy in the western Pacific was most definitely at an end; the *Yamato* and *Yahagi* were both sunk, and four destroyers were sunk as well. The remaining four made it back to the Inland Sea but the end for Japan was now in sight.

Kamikaze attacks were increased on the Allied picket fleet off Okinawa. By 8 April the 6th Marine Division had secured the northern end of Okinawa and was beginning its drive into the Motobu peninsula. The Japanese were in strong defensive positions on the 1500-foot Yae Tae hills. On 14 April the Marines came down on them like hot balls of fire, driving everything before them, so that by 19 April the

Above: *A Marine stands in what is left of a theater in Naha.*
Below: *Japanese troops made a suicidal attempt to destroy Yontan airstrip.*

Left: *Patrols of the 6th Marine Division search for snipers in Naha.*
Right: *Trapped in a cave near Shuri Castle these four Japanese chose to surrender rather than commit suicide.*

entire peninsula was in the hands of the US Marines. The Marines continued to mop up the northern portion of the island until they were redeployed in May to the southern half of the island. The US Army was not making the headway which had been expected of it and Lieutenant General Buckner assumed personal control of the entire operation on 7 May. He redeployed the III Marine Amphibious Force, the 1st and 6th Marine Divisions, to take over the right flank from XXIV Corps which then moved over to the left flank. One action of conspicuous gallantry earned Major Henry Courtney the Medal of Honor. Major Courtney was Executive Officer, Second Battalion, 22nd Marines, 6th Marine Division and was ordered to hold for the night of 14/15 May 1945, in static defense behind Sugar Loaf Hill after leading the advance elements of his command in a prolonged fire fight. Courtney requested permission to make an immediate assault against the enemy positions because he felt that with night falling the advantage of an all-out counterattack lay with the enemy. Permission for the attack was granted, and Courtney briefed his small force and then ordered the advance. Disregarding the danger, he blasted nearby enemy cave positions and machine-gun emplacements. His men, inspired by his leadership and zeal, followed without hesitation. Upon reaching the crest, he waited for more ammunition and reinforcements before continuing. Reinforced by 26 men and an LVT load of grenades, he then drove the remaining enemy off the crest of the hill and ordered his men to dig in.

Courtney was killed instantaneously by a mortar burst while moving his wounded men to safer positions. His unwavering devotion to duty in the face of constant enemy fire was truly in the best tradition of the United States Marine Corps.

Meanwhile the 1st Marine Division had been fighting under the guns of the Shuri hills. Here the 1st Division and the 77th Infantry Division encountered the Wana defenses, northwest of Shuri. Behind the Wana Ridge flowed the Asa River and the deep Wana Gorge. The Japanese had fortified Hill 55 overlooking the Gorge and the Marines had to take it. The 5th and 7th Marines moved against it from opposite sides. The 7th Marines after five days of continuous heavy fighting to take the Ridge lost 51 killed and 387 wounded in action. On 19 May the 1st Marines relieved them. The 1st Marines then immediately assaulted the ridge with grenades and heavy automatic weapons fire and succeeded in taking the crest. By 20 May the 5th Marines had managed to capture the western end of Hill 55 and were moving into the draw. But the Japanese still held 110 Meter Hill, and this made it

Right: A Grumman TBF Avenger begins its bomb run over Okinawa.
Far right: Mopping up operations in a cane field in Okinawa.

virtually impossible for the Marines to advance on Shuri. Then the rains came and turned the entire island into a vast sea of mud through which absolutely nothing could move. By 28 May the rains had stopped and the advance began again. Tuesday, 29 May, witnessed the 1st Battalion, 5th Marines take Shuri Castle. Okinawa was practically secured. So far, Lieutenant General Buckner's Army had sustained 5655 killed and 23,909 wounded in action, while the Japanese had lost over 62,000 dead.

Finally, fresh Marines arrived to bolster up the tired Assault Force; these were Colonel Clarence Walker's, 8th Marines, 2nd Division. By the middle of June the Japanese defenses were really weakening. Lieutenant

Right: Trucks bring the 15th Regiment, 6th Marine Division to the front line at Onayama outside Naha.
Below: More Japanese are prepared to give up the fight against the Marines.

Chance Vought F4U Corsair

This was the first US aircraft to exceed 400 mph in level flight and probably the best US fighter in World War II. It was first ordered in 1941 but did not enter service until 1944 because the US Navy had reservations about its safety and use on carriers. It was unmistakable with its inverted gull wings and cockpit set well at the back. In order to compensate for the restriction in the pilot's view from having the cockpit so far back, Vought adopted a canopy to raise the cockpit. It was an extremely useful fighter with an excellent combat record – by VJ-Day Corsairs had shot down over 2000 enemy aircraft. The cutaway and photographs are of the early version which saw service in the Pacific in 1944–45. Corsairs were such useful aircraft that they were constantly updated and improved and remained in production for 11 years. The F4U-4 saw service in Korea and at that time its maximum speed was 446 mph, with a rate of climb of 7.7 minutes to 20,000 feet.

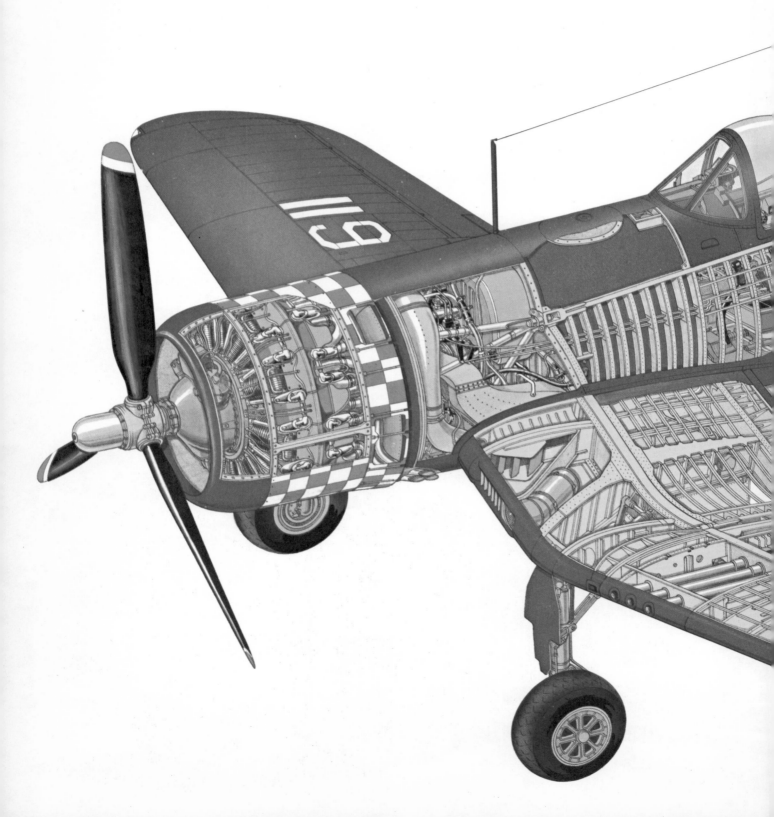

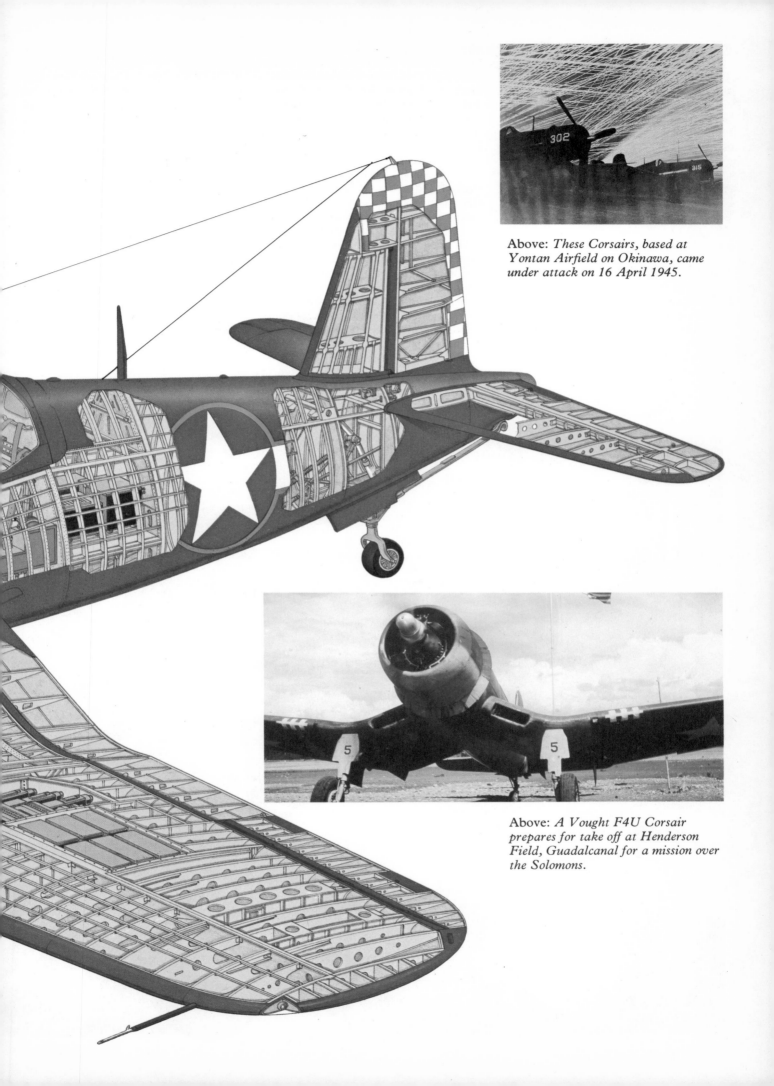

Above: *These Corsairs, based at Yontan Airfield on Okinawa, came under attack on 16 April 1945.*

Above: *A Vought F4U Corsair prepares for take off at Henderson Field, Guadalcanal for a mission over the Solomons.*

General Buckner had previously decided to visit the front to see the 8th Marines go into action. He was witnessing the advance from the 3rd Battalion's observation post when an enemy shell struck nearby and blew a piece of coral into the general's chest. Buckner died soon after. The man who succeeded him was Major General Roy Geiger, a Marine. Geiger became the first Marine officer ever to command an entire field army. On 23 June General Joseph (Vinegar Joe) Stilwell, the ex-commander of the China-Burma-India Theater, was named 10th Army commander. Geiger was promoted to lieutenant general and became commanding general, Fleet Marine Force, Pacific. On 21 June Geiger declared that Okinawa was secure. Marine casualties for the offensive totalled 20,020 of which 3561 were killed.

Okinawa was over but the next destination was mainland Japan. Two major operations were planned: Operation Olympic was the attack on Kyushu and Operation Coronet was the attack on Honshu's Tokyo Plain. All six Marine Corps Divisions were to be utilized in the great assault on Japan. The commander of the entire invasion force, the largest the world had ever seen would be General Douglas MacArthur. However to speed up the end of the war, President Harry Truman ordered the dropping of an atomic device on the city of Hiroshima. On 6 August 1945 Colonel Paul Tibbets in the *Enola Gay*, a B-29 Superfortress, took off from North Field, Tinian and dropped the device on Hiroshima. On 9 August a second bomb was dropped on the industrial city of Nagasaki. Emperor Hirohito surrendered at 0615 hours on 14 August 1945 and the war was finally over.

Right: *1st Lieutenant David Duncan tries to clean the inside of a P-38 belly tank.*
Far right: *The flag is raised over Shuri.*
Below: *Acting Marine Mess Sergeant Corporal Nelson Deffner samples the chow.*

Other medal of honor winners – Pacific campaigns

Name	Location	Date	Unit
Private First Class Harold Agerholm	Saipan	1944	10th Marines
Private First Class Richard Anderson	Kwajalein	1944	23rd Marines
Major Kenneth Bailey	Guadalcanal	1942	1st Raider Battalion
Sergeant John Basilone	Guadalcanal	1942	7th Marines
Lieutenant Colonel Harold Bauer	Guadalcanal	1942	VMF-212
Corporal Lewis Bausell	Peleliu	1944	5th Marines
1st Lieutenant Alexander Bonneyman	Tarawa	1943	18th Marines
Staff Sergeant William Bordelon	Tarawa	1943	18th Marines
Major Gregory Boyington	Central Solomons	1943–44	VMF-214
1st Lieutenant George Cannon	Midway	1941	6th Def Battalion
Corporal Anthony Damato	Eniwetok	1944	22nd Marines
1st Lieutenant Jefferson DeBlanc	Solomons	1943	22nd Marines
Lieutenant-Colonel Aquilla Dyess	Kwajalein	1944	24th Marines
Colonel Merritt Edson	Guadalcanal	1942	1st Raider Battalion
Captain Henry Elrod	Wake Island	1941	VMF-211
Private First Class Harold Epperson	Saipan	1944	6th Marines
Captain Richard Fleming	Midway	1942	VSMB-241
Captain Joseph Foss	Guadalcanal	1942	VMF-121
Major Robert Galer	Solomons	1942	VMF-224
Private First Class Henry Gurke	Bougainville	1943	3rd Raider Battalion
1st Lieutenant Robert Hanson	Rabaul	1943–44	VMF-215
1st Lieutenant William Hawkins	Tarawa	1943	2nd Marines
Private First Class Arthur Jackson	Peleliu	1944	7th Marines
Private Richard Kraus	Peleliu	1944	8th Amphibian Tractor Battalion
Private First Class Leonard Mason	Guam	1944	3rd Marine
Gunnery Sergeant Robert McCard	Saipan	1944	4th Tank Battalion
Private First Class John New	Peleliu	1944	7th Marines
Sergeant Robert Owens	Bougainville	1943	3rd Marines
Private Joseph Ozbourn	Tinian	1944	23rd Marines
Platoon Sergeant Mitchell Paige	Guadalcanal	1942	7th Marines
Private Wesley Phelps	Peleliu	1944	7th Marines
Captain Everett Pope	Peleliu	1944	1st Marines
1st Lieutenant John Power	Kwajalein	1944	24th Marines
Private First Class Charles Roan	Peleliu	1944	7th Marines
2nd Lieutenant Carlton Rouh	Peleliu	1944	5th Marines
Colonel David Shoup	Tarawa	1943	2nd Marines
Private First Class Luther Skaggs	Guam	1944	3rd Marines
Major John Smith	Solomons	1942	VMF-223
Private Richard Sorenson	Kwajalein	1944	24th Marines
1st Lieutenant James Swett	Solomons	1943	VMF-221
Sergeant Herbert Thomas	Bougainville	1943	3rd Marines
Sergeant Clyde Thomason	Makin Island	1942	2nd Raider Battalion
Sergeant Grant Timmerman	Saipan	1944	2nd Tank Battalion
Major General Alexander Vandegrift	Solomons	1942	1st Marine Division
1st Lieutenant Kenneth Walsh	Solomons	1943	VMf-124
Captain Louis Wilson	Guam	1944	9th Marines
Private First Class Robert Wilson	Tinian	1944	6th Marines
Private First Class Frank Witek	Guam	1944	9th Marines

Total: 48

Equipped with scaling ladders Marines head for the seawall at Inchon in Korea, during the second assault of 15 September 1950.

To the Shores of Korea

Japan's Surrender

The war was over but the hardest times were still to come. The US had to occupy Japan and most senior American commanders were worried about the possibility that the Japanese might have a change of heart once they started seeing former enemy combat troops in their homeland. The Japanese offered absolutely no resistance at all; in fact, they seemed very complacent and resigned. The 4th Marines had the honor of leading the US Navy into Japan, as they were the regiment which had been forced to surrender at the very beginning of the war. It was reinforced and became the cornerstone of the Fleet Landing Force. The Fleet Landing Force was composed of the 4th Marines, 2000 Marines from the Third Fleet, a naval regiment of 956 men and 450 British Royal Marines. This force was commanded by Brigadier General William Clement. Clement had served with the old 4th Marines at Shanghai and was evacuated from Corregidor by submarine. His task was to occupy and garrison the Yokosuka Naval base and airfield west of Tokyo Bay. At 0558 hours on 30 August 1945 Major Frank Carney brought the 2nd Battalion, 4th Marines onto the Japanese mainland at Cape Futtsu. The formal surrender ceremonies were conducted on 2 September, a Sunday, in Tokyo Bay, aboard the battleship *Missouri*. Flying from the bridge was the 31-star American flag which had flown from Commodore Perry's flagship when he entered Tokyo Bay in 1853. The colors on the flagstaff were the same which had been flown from the Capitol in Washington on 7 December 1941. MacArthur accepted the formal surrender of Japan as Supreme Allied

Right: *The Japanese surrender ceremony on the USS* Missouri, *MacArthur stands at the table as the Japanese sign.*
Below: *Marines stand at attention as the Japanese Mission leaves the ship.*

Marine corps aces in World War II and the Korean War

No	Name	Number of Planes Shot Down	No	Name	Number of Planes Shot Down
1	Boyington, Gregory	28	66	Dillow, Eugene	6
2	Foss, Joseph	26	67	Dorroh, Jefferson	6
3	Hanson, Robert	26	68	Drury, Frank	6
4	Walsh, Kenneth	21	69	Fisher, Don	6
5	Aldrich, Donald	20	70	Fraser, Robert	6
6	Smith, John	19	71	Freeman, William	6
7	Carl, Marion	18½	72	Hall, Sheldon	6
8	Thomas, Wilbur	18½	73	Hundley, John	6
9	Swett, James	15½	74	Jones, Charles	6
10	Spears, Harold	15	75	McManus, John	6
11	Donahue, Archie	14	76	Percy, Gilbert	6
12	Cupp, James	13	77	Pierce, Francis	6
13	Galer, Robert	13	78	Pond, Zenneth	6
14	Marontate, William	13	79	Presley, Frank	6
15	Shaw, Edward	13	80	Shuman, Perry	6
16	Frazier, Kenneth	12½	81	Stout, Robert	6
17	Everton, Loren	12	82	Terrill, Francis	6
18	Segal, Harold	12	83	Valentine, Herbert	6
19	Trowbridge, Eugene	12	84	Vedder, Milton	6
20	†Bolt, John	12	85	Hansen, Herman	5½
21	DeLong, Philip	11⅙	86	Hood, William	5½
22	Bauer, Harold	11	87	Kirkpatrick, Floyd	5½
23	Sapp, Donald	11	88	Lundin, William	5½
24	Conger, Jack	10½	89	Payne, Frederick	5½
25	Long, Herbert	10	90	Sigler, Wallace	5⅓
26	DeBlanc, Jefferson	9	91	Alley, Stuart	5
27	Magee, Christopher	9	92	Baldwin, Frank	5
28	Mann, Thomas	9	93	Braun, Richard	5
			94	Carlton, William	5
30	Thomas, Franklin	9	95	Davis, Leonard	5
31	Loesch, Gregory	8½	96	Dawkins, George	5
32	Morgan, John	8½	97	Doyle, Cecil	5
33	Snider, William	8½	98	Drake, Charles	5
34	Case, William	8	99	Elwood, Hugh Mc	5
35	Dobbin, John	8	100	Farrell, William	5
36	Gutt, Fred	8	101	Finn, Howard	5
37	Hernan, Edwin	8	102	Fontana, Paul	5
38	Hollowell, George	8	103	Ford, Kenneth	5
39	Kunz, Charles	8	104	Hacking, Albert	5
40	Narr, Joseph	8	105	Kendrick, Charles	5
41	Post, Nathan	8	106	Laird, Wayne	5
42	Warner, Arthur	8	107	McCartney, Henry	5
43	Yost, Donald	8	108	McGinty, Selva	5
44	Baker, Robert	7	109	Olander, Edwin	5
45	*Brown, William	7	110	Phillips, Hyde	5
46	Caswell, Dean	7	111	Poske, George	5
47	Crowe, William	7	112	Powell, Ernest	5
48	Haberman, Roger	7	113	Ramlo, Orvin	5
49	Hamilton, Henry	7	114	Scarborough, Hartwell	5
50	Jensen, Alvin	7	115	Scherer, Raymond	5
51	McClurg, Robert	7	116	See, Robert	5
52	O'Keefe, Jeremiah	7	117	Synar, Stanley	5
53	Owens, Robert	7	118	Weissenberger, Gregory	5
54	Pittman, Jack	7	119	Wells, Albert	5
55	Reinburg, Joseph	7	120	Yunck, Michael	5
56	Ruhsam, John	7	121	Balch, Donald	5
57	Wade, Robert	7	122	Porter, Robert	5
58	Williams, Gerard	7	123	‡Andre, John	5
59	Mullen, Paul	6½			
60	Durnford, Dewey	6⅓			997⅙
61	Dillard, Joseph	6⅓			
62	Axtell, George	6			
63	Baird, Robert	6			
64	Chandler, Creighton	6			
65	Conant, Arthur	6			

*Includes six shot down with the Flying Tigers in China
†Six in WW II and six in Korean war
‡Four in WW II and one in Korean war
¹Official list bears no entry under 29

Above: *Major General Geiger holds the commemorative card produced for those at Japanese surrender ceremony.*

Island and the first man ashore was Colonel Walter Bayler. Bayler was known as "the last man of Wake Island." The commanding general of the 4th Marine Aircraft Wing, Lawson Sanderson, received the surrender of over 1200 Japanese military and naval personnel. Thus the scene of the Marines' first historic defense of the war was rightly reoccupied by Marines once again. The war was over and all the troops wanted to do was go home.

The Cold War

The war was over but the Cold War was only just starting. In the aftermath of the war 53,000 US Marines were ordered into North China in the fall of 1945. These Marines were to ensure that the Japanese armies surrendered. Although this was the primary reason given for dispatching troops to China, the ulterior motive was to combat the already growing power of the Chinese Communists. A line had been drawn in Europe to distinguish between the Communist and non-Communist blocs, but no such clear division was visible in Asia.

The United States backed General Chiang Kai-shek and his Nationalist armies. However Chiang managed to alienate the Chinese people even more than he had already done with his American-supported armies. He behaved like a two-bit gangster in Chicago during the 1920s. He had the temperament of a tyrant and could not bear to have his judgment questioned. The Chinese people on the whole backed the Communist-led armies of Mao Tse-tung. The battle between

Commander Pacific, Nimitz and Halsey represented the Navy at this historic occasion. Lieutenant General Geiger was the Marine Corps' representative.

Meanwhile things were starting to roll in Japan. Colonel John Munn arrived at Yokosuka on 7 September from Okinawa with MAG-31. Things went smoothly for all concerned. The primary task was to rehabilitate the prisoners from the Japanese prisoner of war camps. This was done as speedily and painlessly as possible. By early 1946 the 1st and 2nd Battalions, 4th Marines were home, while the headquarters unit joined the 6th Marines at Tsingtao, China. The 3rd Battalion was left behind at Yokosuka to act as a guard battalion. The 2nd and 5th Marine Divisions occupied Kyushu under Major General Harry Schmidt's V Amphibious Corps. On 4 September 1945 the Marines returned to Wake

these two groups continued for over four years. Meanwhile the Marines remained in China throughout the long and bitter internal struggle, and as usual succeeded in alienating the people even more. The presence of the Marines in North China was a definite check on the Communist attempts to take control.

The III Amphibious Corps commanded by Major General Keller Rockey was the main Marine element stationed in China. On 30 September 1945 the 1st Marine Division landed at Tangku and moved immediately to the Marines' old stomping grounds at Tientsin-Peking. Eleven days later the 6th Marine Division landed at Tsingtao, on the Shantung Peninsula. These two divisions came under the operational control of Lieutenant General

Left: *Recruits arrive at Parris Island.*
Below: *The Brewster F2A-1 Buffalo, a single-engine, one-crew fighter.*

Newly arrived recruits at Parris Island, the Marine Corps Recruit Depot, draw their clothing allowance.

Albert Wedemeyer, Commander of all US forces in China. The Communists did not waste any time with the invaders but immediately initiated attacks against Marine units guarding communications lines, roads and supply depots. Chiang launched an offensive into Manchuria hoping to utilize the Marines as a mobile power base. The Marines were in an ambiguous position and made their feelings known.

The US Ambassador to China, Patrick Hurley resigned on 27 November and President Truman appointed a man for whom he had the greatest respect, General of the Army George Marshall, to be his special envoy to China. On 14 November Major General DeWitt Peck, commander of the 1st Marine Division, was *en route* to Chinwangtao when his train was ambushed by Communist troops. Undeterred Peck started out again the very next day only to find that over 200 yards of track had been destroyed. A Chinese railroad gang was brought up for repairs but they only succeeded in activating a land mine which killed several of them. Peck decided to fly into Chinwangtao. The Marines were forced to aid the Nationalist troops as the fighting became even heavier. They provided the Nationalists with ammunition, weapons, and supplies. Upon Marshall's arrival in Chungking, the fighting halted between the Communists and Nationalists. Newsmen announced that peace was on the horizon in China. Little did they know what was behind the scenes of power. By the

first week of January 1946 the US Marine Corps' total strength was only 301,700, of whom 45,981 were serving in North China. After looking into the troop commitment to China, Marshall ordered that 9200 Marines be sent home. This 20 percent reduction was welcomed openly by Marine Corps HQ as Marine strength was very thin and being stretched even thinner by continued commitments around the globe. Marshall stated on more than one occasion that the Marines represented an embarrassment to his peace negotiations. He hoped that the Nationalists would provide security forces once they realized that the Marines were really leaving. The opposite happened. Chiang's armies crossed into Man-

churia in April and the fighting resumed where it had left off, only heavier than before. The Marines were continually being reduced in strength but still did not lose any of their commitments in China. In July the Communists were on the offensive, their forces were reorganized into the People's Liberation Army and a demand for the withdrawal of all American forces from China was made. Throughout the next two years the Communists fought and seemed to be winning where it mattered. In July 1948, as the Soviets were testing the resolve of the Western Powers over Berlin, the Chinese Communists were advancing not only into northern China but central China as well. The tide was now turning and the Nationalists were beginning to lose credibility. By November 1948 the Nationalists had lost over 400,000 troops and millions of dollars in American supplies. Finally the Battle of Hwai-Hai, the massive 65-day fight, was won by the Communists, who quickly moved onto Peking and Tientsin. The Marines, now commanded by Brigadier General Gerald Thomas, spent their time insuring the safe evacuation of American citizens from China. The complete and total defeat of the Nationalists was sealed at Hwai-Hai. Tsingtao was inevitably doomed and the 9th Marines redeployed to the Whampoa River at Shanghai. By 3

Right: *This recruiting poster was produced in 1947.*
Below: *From 1901 until the present the US has retained a naval base at Guantanamo Bay, Cuba. Sergeant James Easterline and Private 1st Class Eugene Vereb buy bananas off duty.*

February 1949 the remaining Marines in China were all on board transports, except for one company which was acting as a shore patrol unit and picking up any stragglers. On 26 May the last Marines in China were pulled out. The entire fiasco cost the Marines 10 killed and 33 wounded in action. It was the end of an era for the Marines in China. But a new commitment was about to be made in a small backwater peninsular country of little actual value to the USA, a country which Douglas MacArthur and Dean Acheson had stated was beyond the perimeter of US military defenses, although not out of the responsibility of the United Nations. This was Korea. Its roots lay in American Cold War policy which can be best explained by one word – "containment." The US went out of its way in an attempt to contain Communism; the Truman Doctrine, the Marshall Plan, the Rio Treaty and NATO were all parts of US foreign policy.

Korea was turned from a backwater into the focal point of the Cold War, and as such became the keystone of America's containment policy. The Communists had to be stopped no matter where they attempted to expand, and the US was the self-appointed champion of democracy. In June 1950 Korea had nothing to offer except illiteracy, poverty, epidemics and an authoritarian government. For over 100 years it had been a pawn in major Far Eastern power struggles. In 1905 Japan established a protectorate over Korea and in 1910 annexed it.

Above: *Another recruiting poster from the postwar period.*
Below: *Landing craft, carrying men of the 1st Marine Division, head for the beach at Inchon on 15 September 1950.*

After World War II it became a testing ground for foreign policy of the USSR and the USA. This was the setting for the beginning of the Korean War before the major powers became involved in Korean internal affairs.

Korea

On 25 June 1950 the uneasy peace of the postwar period was shattered when the Communist troops of North Korea invaded South Korea. This was the spark which turned the cold war into a raging inferno. It became the first major confrontation on the Asian mainland between the US and militant communism.

Ten superbly trained divisions of the North Korean Army, supported by 500 Soviet tanks and 2000 artillery pieces, mauled and overran South Korean outposts along the border in a massive surprise onslaught. The 100,000-man strong South Korean Army was originally designed by the US as a constabulary force. It was equipped with only small arms and was no match for the highly efficient invading force. The majority of South Korean defenses along the 38th parallel border were smashed in a lightning pre-dawn attack. In only four days the Communist forces captured Seoul, the capital of South Korea, and continued on their drive south toward the sea.

At the end of World War II, when Korea was liberated from Japanese occupation, the country was divided into two parts, the Soviets occupying the north and the US the south. The offensive against South Korea was a first-class example of the enormous amount of arms and training the Soviets were providing their Communist satellites. MacArthur and Secretary of State Dean Acheson had stated that Korea was beyond the perimeter of US military defenses, but not outside the realm of United Nations responsibility. It was obvious from the start that the South Koreans would not be able to stem the Communist advance without direct outside intervention.

President Truman and Acheson assumed the invasion was Soviet directed and possibly the beginning of an extensive Sino-Soviet thrust. Nevertheless their initial reaction was carefully measured. In Tokyo MacArthur was ordered to dispatch supplies to the South Korean troops. Truman then followed up with a containment action, moving the US 7th Fleet between China and Formosa, and sending further assistance to the counter-revolutionary forces in Indo-China and the Philippines. Immediately after the invasion the United Nations Security Council convened, and an American resolution branding North Korea as an aggressor and requesting a withdrawal behind the 38th parallel was passed unopposed, with Yugoslavia abstaining. But the Soviet Union was not represented, as Ambassador Yakov Malik was boycotting the Security Council to protest at the exclusion of Red China. Meanwhile the situation in South Korea was steadily declining. Truman committed American air and naval units into action to stop the flood.

On 27 June, the United Nations passed a resolution recommending immediate aid in restoring peace in South Korea. This was passed seven in favor with Egypt and India abstaining and Yugoslavia against. Ambassador Malik was still not present to exercise his country's veto; the rapidity and forcefulness of Truman's actions had completely surprised the Soviets. The Soviets never again missed a Security Council vote in which their interests were so clearly at stake. The US was named as the executive agent to carry out the UN effort.

Three days later President Truman ordered General MacArthur, in Tokyo, to utilize American ground units to help repel the invaders from South Korean soil. At this point, men of the US Marine Corps were once again called upon to fight and die for their country.

Douglas MacArthur made a surprise visit to the front on 30 June and found that out of an expected 98,000-man Republic of Korea army, only 25,000 were actually effectives. He subsequently recommended in the strongest terms to President Truman that US combat troops be committed to battle. Truman approved this request and an army regimental combat team was dispatched from MacArthur's under-strength four divisions pulling occupa-

tion duties in Japan. By that night the US was fully committed to the defense of the Republic of Korea. On 1 July Lieutenant Colonel Charles Smith and 406 men from the 1st Battalion, 21st Infantry were on their way to Korea. Task Force Smith, now with 450 men, went into battle on 5 July in the rain and were soundly trounced above Osan by two North Korean regular regiments and 33 tanks. The next day was no better for US ground operations; the 34th Infantry had two battalions scattered to the wind when they moved up to cover Smith's original positions. Committing relatively small combat forces against a numerically superior enemy was neither rational nor realistic, and consequently losses were high and totally unnecessary.

Above: *Marines move out of Inchon past a burning North Korean tank.*
Far right: *A Marine with a 3.5 bazooka tries to blast Communist forces out of their position on a hill, September 1950.*
Below: *In one of the fastest amphibious operations ever, the Marines used scaling ladders to achieve the maximum surprise at Inchon.*

Pusan Perimeter

The first Marines to land in Korea were a demolition party from the cruiser *Juneau*, consisting of one officer and four enlisted men. They went ashore in a whaleboat from the destroyer *Mansfield* to plant two 60-pound explosive charges in a railroad tunnel south of Chongjin. The rapid build up of American strength was impressive but extremely expensive. On 8 July 1950 President Truman named General Douglas MacArthur as Commander of the United Nations Forces in Korea. Lieutenant General

Walton Walker took command of the US 8th Army forces in Korea on 13 July. On 20 July the 24th Infantry Division defending Taejon was practically annihilated, it lost over 30 percent of its assigned 12,200 troops. The commander of the 24th Infantry was Major General William Dean, who was captured and held prisoner by the North Koreans for over three years. Now the remnants of the 24th, the understrength 25th Infantry Division and 1st Air Cavalry Division with only

39,000 troops were thrown into the southeastern portion of Korea in a defensive perimeter around the port of Pusan. This pocket of resistance was only 100 miles deep and 50 miles wide. The race was on, the North Koreans intent on only one thing – the total destruction of the American Forces and the remainder of the South Korean Army. Reinforcements were on the way from the US but the question that Walker had to face was would they arrive in time to save his men from

North Korean prisoners are escorted by South Koreans and a Marine tank to the nearest stockade in September 1950.

154

Above: *Chinese troops wearing inadequate footwear surrender to Charley Company, 7th Marines south of Koto-ri.*
Below: *Icy temperatures and lashing winds slow down the Marines as they return from Koto-ri to the sea.*

certain destruction. The USAF did everything in its power to slow the enemy advance. Continuous air strikes were launched around the clock against enemy troop concentrations, supply depots and lines of supply. Lieutenant General Walker, on 29 July 1950, ordered the 8th Army to halt its retreat and to hold its ground or die trying. This was the predicament of the forces defending the Pusan perimeter; hold or die. Walker stated, "A Marine force, and two regiments are expected in the next few days to reinforce us. . . . There is no line behind us in which we can

retreat. . . . There will be no Dunkirk, there will be no Bataan. . . . We must fight until the end. . . . We are going to hold this line. We are going to win." The North Koreans attempted an enveloping maneuver but were held at the Naktong River. By 5 August there were 47,000 US troops in Korea. USAF planes were blowing up bridges, railroads and troop concentrations. Finally, the UN Command took the offensive. Major General William Kean ordered the 35th Infantry, the 5th Regimental Combat Team and the 1st Marine Provisional Brigade forward to attack the North Korean 6th Division southwest of Masan.

MacArthur had asked for a Marine combat team back in July and they landed at Pusan on 2 August, anxious for a piece of the action. This brigade was under the command of Brigadier General Edward Craig who had won the Navy Cross at Guam. The commander of MAG-33 was Brigadier General Thomas Cushman. This command totalled 6534 men. The key unit in the command was the 5th Marines who had fought at Belleau Wood, Nicaragua, Guadalcanal, New Britain, Peleliu and Okinawa. The 1st Battalion, 11th Marines was the brigade's artillery.

On 10 July Lieutenant General Shepard, Commander Fleet Marines, Pacific and his adviser, Colonel Victor

Above: *Marines drive forward after effective close air support from Vought F4U Corsairs. The 1st Marine Division was fighting in the vicinity of Hagaru-ri in December 1950.*

Left: *After fighting in appalling weather conditions, the 5th and 7th Marines hear the welcome news that they are to be withdrawn. They had fought all the way down the road to Hagaru and then to the sea in December 1950.*
Right: *Marines clear the way for a new position in March 1951.*
Below: *The HTL-4 Trainer helicopter was used for observation and liaison missions.*

Krulak, flew into Tokyo for a conference with the UN commander. MacArthur then laid his strategy in front of the Marine officers. He planned to take the enemy by surprise by landing an entire Marine division behind their lines and cutting them off from their base and supplies. It was a daring plan, a fantasy of strategy, only a madman could have concocted it; the difference was that the genius who thought it up was the mastermind behind the American military victory in the Pacific and the greatest military strategist in American history. Shepard told MacArthur that the 1st Marine Division could be ready for the amphibious operation by 15 September at Inchon.

Meanwhile on the home front, President Truman acting on recommendations from the Joint Chiefs of Staff, called up 33,000 Marines from the Organized Marine Corps Reserve. By 7 August the 50,000 Marines of the Volunteer Reserve were all notified they would be called up as well. The Marine Brigade was on its way to Japan to get ready for MacArthur's counterattack, but they were diverted straight into Korea. The North Koreans, seeing the end in sight, were closing the gap around Pusan and were throwing in everything they had. The Marines unloaded in the dark on 2 August. Carrying field pack, rifle, ammunition and rations, the Marines were deployed to the area adjacent to Changwon.

The first American offensive was ready to be launched from Chindong-ni to Chinji. The Marines would circle to the southwest, the 35th Infantry would hit the enemy from the northeast, and the 5th Regimental Combat Team would move straight westward

158

through the center. This attack began on the eighth anniversary of the landings on Guadalcanal. The men of the 3rd Battalion, 5th Marines, under Lieutenant Colonel Robert Taplett, dug in on Hill 255 on 6 August. F Company, 5th Infantry was holding Hill 342 and was in dire need of reinforcements. Taplett was ordered to send help. He dispatched 2nd Lieutenant John Cahill with G Company to Hill 342. After making their way through intense enemy artillery fire and being fired on by the US Army, the Marines finally made it to the hill. Cahill and Sergeant Lee Buettner went forward to ascertain where the army unit was located, and were fired upon by the enemy. Of the 52 Marines who set out to reach the hill, only 37 made it to the summit. Three Marines were killed and eight wounded in action. The North Koreans then surrounded the hill. An airdrop was attempted but crucial supplies of water and food fell into the hands of the enemy. The 2nd Marine Battalion went forward to

break through, but it was not until the following day that D and E Companies arrived. Fighting continued over Hill 342 until on 9 August, the 24th Infantry took over. The Marines were now pushing south; the 1st Battalion took Hill 308 and secured the Tosan road junction which was of vital importance to the advance. The 2nd Battalion, commanded by Lieutenant Colonel Harold Roise ran into an ambush nine miles from Kosong in the narrow Taedabok Pass. Meanwhile Taplett's 3rd Battalion had leapfrogged past this obstacle and was in a good forward position. The Marines were moving ahead, and with Taedabok Pass secured headed for Sachon. Kosong was entered by H Company in the company of two Pershing M-26 tanks. On 12 August the enemy took two hills on both sides of the valley at Changchon village and tried to pull off an ambush of a Marine column. The trap would have worked except that Captain Kenneth Houghton's Reconnaissance Company prematurely ac-

Above right: Leathernecks of the 1st Marine Division test new winter clothing while on exercises.
Below: A Marine Corps 105 mm howitzer crew in action on the central front in Korea.

tivated it. Houghton's men were about one mile in front of B Company who also drew enemy fire. Tanks were called for immediately to help in dislodging the North Koreans from their emplacements on the two hills. Captain Tobin, B Company commander sent the 1st Platoon to reinforce the Recon Company, and the 3rd Platoon to hit the hill on the right from which the attack on the Reconnaissance Company had come. The 3rd Platoon took this hill with ease but the enemy regrouped on the opposite face and without any warning launched a counterattack. The Marines were in their turn driven half way down the reverse slope. A Company then attacked the hill on the right and managed to take the top by 1700 hours. B Company assaulted Hill 202 and took it by 2000 hours. The Marines had quite a lot to be proud of; in four days they had driven the North Koreans back 22 miles, but for all their pains the Marines were without water or rations.

The Brigade was now engaged on two fronts over 25 miles apart. Brigadier General Craig maintained firm operational control over his

this period, Marine losses were 172 killed and 730 wounded in action. The Brigade was transferred to Pusan to await a pick up. On 13 September the 1st Provincial Marine Brigade was deactivated and its units were amalgamated with the 1st Marine Division. The next destination was Inchon.

Inchon

MacArthur's strategy was beginning to unfold: although his UN Command was pinned down to a small corner of Korea surrounding Pusan, he built a second assault force to carry the fight where the enemy would least expect it. All the experts and tacticians, from the Army, Navy and even the Marines attempted to change his mind, arguing that the risks entailed in this type of amphibious operation would be extremely great. His force would have to manage its way through the narrow channel during the three-day period in the month when the tides were high enough to carry the landing craft over the Inchon harbor walls. MacArthur had made his mind up and nothing and absolutely no one would change it. Quite a few individuals tried to: the Army Chief of Staff, Chief of Naval Operation, the Commander of the Pacific Fleet Marines, but with no success. MacArthur was 70 years old and arguably the greatest general the US produced. On 23 August admirals and generals gathered at his headquarters, the Dai Ichi Building in Tokyo, to talk about the hazards, shortage of time, and numerous other items which they felt would result in the operation becoming a failure. Impervious to all the criticism MacArthur spoke to them for 45 minutes, explaining exactly what he planned to do and the immense psychological advantages of his masterpiece of strategic insight. He concluded: "We shall land at Inchon, and I shall crush them."

The amphibious landing would be accomplished by the X Corps consisting of the 1st Marine Division and would be followed by the Army 7th Infantry Division. The Marines hoped that MacArthur would select Lieutenant General Shepard as the overall commander for the entire operation, but the man selected was MacArthur's Chief of Staff, Major General Edward Almond. The reason for this selection is rather obscure and will never really be known. The greatest problem facing

separated forces by helicopter. The Brigade was ordered to pull back for redeployment in another sector. The first offensive had accomplished its objective, the halting of the 6th North Korean Division. Moving 75 miles by rail, the Marines ate their first hot meal in over 13 days and managed to change their rotten uniforms. They now came under the operational control of the 24th Infantry Division, commanded by Brigadier General John Church. Everything was now set for the Battle of Naktong.

The Naktong River was the last natural barrier west of the Pusan Perimeter; once it was crossed the enemy had a clear run to Pusan itself. On 6 August North Korean troops started to ferry across the river. This offensive endangered an important objective, the lifeline from Taegu, the provincial capital. The enemy came over in strength at the Naktong Bulge, an area east of the river, west of Miryang and Yongsan, and four miles by five. The river bends westward around a mass of hills, the most suitable for occupation being Hill 311. On the east side of this formation were two hills: the Cloverleaf Hill and Obong-ni Ridge. By 10 August the entire 4th North Korean Division had crossed the Naktong, overrun the Bulge and were on their way east. The UN Forces were in a sorry situation. By 18 August Taegu was evacuated and the South Korean government was relocated in Pusan.

Colonel John Hill's Task Force of three Army infantry regiments attempted to stop the North Korean advance, but to absolutely no avail. General Walker knew that this North Korean offensive had to be stopped at

all costs. He told Church, "I'm giving you the Marine Brigade; clean this mess up and quick." The counterattack was initiated on 17 August: the 19th and 34th Infantry Regiments hit the enemy from the northeast, the 21st Infantry was partially blocked on the southern fringe, and the Marine Brigade and what was left of the 9th Combat Regimental Team moved west directly through the center along the Yongsan-Naktong road. On the left the Marines assaulted No Name Ridge (formerly called Obong-ni Ridge), while the 9th RCT covered them; this role was to be reversed for the attack on Cloverleaf Hill. The entire attack was mismanaged from the start. Flank support was lacking; artillery support was not properly co-ordinated; the air strikes from the carriers were over 15 minutes late; and the cost was heavy. Out of 240 men, 2nd Battalion, 5th Marines, 142 men were either killed or wounded before the end of the day. After taking No Name Ridge, the Marines' next objective was Hill 207, just west of the Ridge. Taplett's 3rd Battalion took it by the morning of the 18 August. The entire Naktong Bulge was now full of retreating North Korean troops trying to get back across the river to safety. American victory turned rapidly into a slaughter. The enemy was caught by artillery, mortar and aircraft fire, and killed in such numbers as to change the color of the river. This battle must rank as one of the hardest fought in the annals of Marine Corps history.

In three major operations in one calendar month, the Marines had been a major factor in stopping the North Korean invasion and saving the Pusan Perimeter from being overrun. During

MacArthur's landing was lack of time. Inchon has the most extraordinary tides in the entire world. The landing had to be made in two phases. The Marines had to secure Wolmi-do Island in the harbor on the morning of the landings. This was to be accomplished by the 3rd Battalion, 5th Marines. While this was going on, the 1st Marines and the remainder of the 5th would take the city itself on the evening tide, which was more difficult than it seemed. Once the main landing was completed, the Marines would have only two hours to get all their equipment and men ashore. Marine Corsairs flew combat photo reconnaissance missions of the strike zone. Wolmi-do Island was hit by naval and air attacks for five straight days to soften it up for the Marine landing force. The last possible danger to MacArthur's Inchon operation was ignored when Rear Admiral James Doyle put the invasion fleet to sea one

Right: After the end of hostilities, the Marines remained to garrison South Korea.
Below: Marine Sergeant Ireland leads his patrol back to the front.

day early to evade Typhoon Kezia and her 125 mph winds. The flagship of Task Force 90 put in at Sasebo, Japan to pick up MacArthur and his personal advisers. Lieutenant General Shepard was his amphibious adviser. Besides the 1st Marine Division, there were 3000 men of the 1st Korean Marine Corps Regiment and 2700 specialized US Army troops, which brought the total strength of the landing force to 25,040 men. In an unprecedented move, the Secretary of the Navy ordered the removal of some 500 Marines from the invasion force who were under 18 years of age. The fleet led by the destroyer *Mansfield* sailed down the narrow passage to Inchon, aided by the beacon on Palmi-do Island (this was accomplished by Lieutenant Eugene Clark, who two weeks before D-Day landed with two South Koreans to gather information and to relight the beacon at Palmi-do Island). Friday, 15 September 1950 was D-Day, it was a warm and quite enjoyable day. It started off with Marine and Navy carrier-based aircraft hitting enemy targets. Taplett's G Company and a further three platoons

Right: Marines bring in two North Korean soldiers who had changed into civilian clothes before capture.
Below: Crewmen of a battery unit watch anxiously as the helicopter brings ammunition in special baskets.

of H Company landed on the northwest section of Wolmi-do. The rest of his men arrived two minutes later. G Company under 1st Lieutenant Robert Bohn headed straight for Radio Hill, where all the North Korean troops surrendered. By 0655 hours Sergeant Alvin Smith, 3rd Platoon Guide, G Company raised the flag on the crest of Radio Hill. MacArthur, watching for some sign from the island, saw the flag and said, "That's it. Let's get a cup of coffee." He immediately dispatched a message throughout the Task Force: "The Navy and Marines have never shone more brightly than this morning." By 1000 hours Taplett's men had captured the adjacent island of Sowolmi-do which was linked to

Wolmi-do by a 750-yard causeway. Three Marines were wounded so far but none had been killed. By 1300 hours the tide had receded, trapping over 1000 Marines on their captured islands.

The main landings were now begun. Newton's 1st and Roise's 2nd Battalions, 5th Marines landed in the center of Inchon at Red Beach. They were ordered to take Cemetery Hill and Observatory Hill and then advance through the city. Chesty Puller's 1st Marines landed at Blue Beach which was situated in the industrial portion of the city. By the end of the day, everything had gone off as MacArthur had planned – the landing was a success. At this stage, there were

13,000 US troops ashore. Marine casualties for D-Day were extremely light considering what had been expected, only 22 killed and 174 wounded in action, plus 14 non-combat casualties.

"I have just returned from visiting the Marines at the front, and there is not a finer fighting organization in the world."
Douglas MacArthur
Outskirts of Seoul, 21 September 1950

Over the Yalu River

Throughout the rest of September and early October the Marines assaulted enemy positions, attacked and took Seoul. By 5 October 1950 the Marines had been ordered to return to Inchon where a military cemetery was dedicated to their fallen comrades in battle. On 7 October the amphibious operation was concluded and the Marines were being redeployed to Wonsan and a different type of war altogether. The entire Inchon-Seoul campaign was executed with daring and speed. The actual landings at Inchon went off in text-book style. Seoul fell in two weeks. The cost to the 1st Marine Division was 421 killed and 2029 wounded in action. North Korean losses were 13,666 and 4692 prisoners. MacArthur's report to the UN termed the campaign as "decisive." He had saved the day once again when all seemed lost.

The next act in the play was just beginning to unfold: a decision had been made to cross the 38th Parallel; the major focus should have been on attempting to find a process to remove or avoid the uncertainty which the decision caused. What had happened was that generals were playing at International Relations, and were trying to simplify the decision-making process. This decision to cross the 38th Parallel was a major turning point because without taking into consideration all the possible hypothetical consequences of that momentous decision, the US was brought into direct confrontation with the People's Republic of China, which produced the ultimate defeat of American arms in Korea. It was a root cause of McCarthyite fear and frustration through the 1950s. It encouraged nationalism in the Asian countries and Communist China was raised to the status of defender of the faith – Communism. It left the US in a state of internal turmoil for a decade. Dean

Acheson called it "the greatest defeat suffered by American arms since the Battle of Manassas and an international disaster of the first order." But the decision firmly rested with President Harry Truman and on 27 September the Joint Chiefs of Staff with presidential approval gave MacArthur these orders:

Your military objective is the destruction of the North Korean Armed Forces. In attaining this objective you are authorized to conduct military operations, including amphibious and airborne landings or ground operations north of the 38th Parallel in Korea, provided that at the time of such operations there has been no entry into North Korea by major Soviet or Chinese Communist Forces, no announcements of intended entry, nor a threat to counter our operations militarily in North Korea . . . under no circumstances, however, will your forces cross the Manchurian or USSR borders of Korea and, as a matter of policy, no non-Korean Ground Forces will be used in the northeast provinces bordering the Soviet Union or in the area along the Manchurian border. Furthermore, support of your operations north or south of the 38th Parallel will not include Air or Naval action against Manchuria or against USSR territory.

A plan was developed for the 8th Army to drive north as far as Pyongyang, the capital of North Korea, and for the X Corps to trap the North Korean forces retreating from the south by making a landing at Wonsan. Both forces would then join up and advance to positions 50 and 100 miles below the border of Manchuria. If any units were needed to advance further than this predetermined line, they would be South Korean, ROK forces. ROK units began moving across the parallel on 1 October. President Rhee was determined to unite Korea, but the Chinese had other things in mind. Chou En-lai, Prime Minister of China warned the Indian ambassador in Peking that if US troops crossed the Parallel, China would enter the war. On 7 October the 8th Army attacked North Korean positions across the Parallel and now the die had been cast. MacArthur met with President Truman and his staff at the famous Wake Island conference. The general assured Truman that victory was close at hand. In reply to Truman's specific questions about the possibility of indirect or direct Chinese or Soviet intervention, MacArthur reassured him that there was no likelihood of

such a clash. He went even further to say that if the Chinese deployed a massive number of ground units across the Yalu, they would be annihilated by air power before they could reach Pyongyang. He went further and predicted troop withdrawals by Christmas. Truman left Wake Island satisfied that everything had been adequately settled by his Field Commander and himself.

MacArthur truly did not believe that the Chinese would step in, and thought if they did he would utterly destroy them with massive air strikes. He did not know that 120,000 Communist

Chinese troops were in front of the X Corps and a further 180,000 more in front of the 8th Army – one cannot ignore 300,000 veteran soldiers. In early November Marine reconnaissance pilots of VMF(N)-542 reported that large groups of trucks were moving from China into Korea. MacArthur immediately requested Truman's permission to destroy the bridges over the Yalu. Truman first refused, but after incessant arguments from his general, gave in to the demand. The President stipulated that under no circumstances would power plants or dams be hit, and he refused

MacArthur permission to carry out "hot pursuit" across the Manchurian border against MiG fighters. The scene was ready for a confrontation between two of the world's great powers.

By 20 October Pyongyang fell to the US forces. The war was just about over and the boys were to go home for Christmas. MacArthur then ordered his front lines to be moved to within 30–40 miles of the Manchurian border, and simultaneously ordered Lieutenant General Walker and Major General Almond to occupy all of North Korea. The Joint Chiefs queried his

orders but his reply must have been sufficient because no one in staff authority had the courage to countermand one of the "old man's" orders. A direct result of these new orders was that the Marines were ordered to relieve the I ROK Corps at the Chosin and Fusen Reservoirs. Throughout the rest of October and into November the Marines moved North, assaulting enemy positions, protecting supply

Marine artillerymen fire support for infantrymen fighting Chinese troops near Hongchon, 50 miles west of Seoul, the South Korean capital.

dumps and defending strategic hill locations. The 1st Marines were engaged at Kojo, Majon-ni and Muchon-ni. The 5th and 7th Marines were continuing to advance to the Manchurian border. Back at HQ, MacArthur had divided his army, making the 8th Army and X Corps separate operating commands. In doing this, his commands were split by the Taebaek Mountain Range, which ran down the length of the Korean peninsula. To make matters worse, there were no passable roads through the mountains running east to west, north of Wonsan and Pyongyang. MacArthur did not want to relinquish control of the entire ground force to Walker and this was a primary consideration in his retaining Almond as his X Corps commander. Almond was also retained as his deputy Chief of Staff.

Meanwhile the Chinese had crossed the Yalu with 180,000 troops and were within 50 miles of North Korea. They were well camouflaged, moved with great skill and always stopped two hours or more before dawn to hide their positions and equipment. The Thirteenth Army Group, commanded by General Lin Piao had assembled in forward concentration areas north of the Chongchon River, from near Chongju in the west to the Chosin reservoir in the east. They were now ready to take on the 8th Army. In a line 150 miles long, the 38th, 39th, 40th, 42nd, 50th and 66th Armies of three divisions each were concealed and waiting for the word to attack the Americans in a complete surprise move. In November they were re-inforced by the Ninth Army Group of General Chen Yi's Third Field Army, composed of the 20th, 26th and 27th Armies, each of four divisions. This force was concentrated to strike the flank of the X Corps near the Chosin and Fusen Reservoirs. The Chinese and North Korean forces had the US troops outnumbered two to one, and had the key element of surprise in their favor.

The advance was well underway and MacArthur's grand design was about to be shattered. The Marines were moving steadily toward the Manchurian border. On 2 November the 7th Marines relieved the 26th ROK Regiment, 37 miles north of Hungnam

at Majon-dong on the Main Supply Route (MSR). Some Chinese troop concentrations had been spotted numbering over 500 men. At dusk the Marines halted and dug in at a bridge about a mile south of Sudong. Colonel Litzenberg ordered the 1st Battalion to place its rifle companies on the high ground in front and the 2nd Battalion on the slopes near the center. The 3rd Battalion guarded the rear. The Marines were totally unaware that the Chinese had their 371st Regiment to the north, 372nd Regiment directly in front of them and the 370th Regiment to the east. This was a sizable force for only one Marine regiment to take on practically single-handed. At 2300 hours two Chinese battalions attacked in a double enveloping maneuver. By 0100 hours 3 November, the Marine 1st and 2nd Battalions were being hit on both flanks. The Chinese were everywhere. They quickly overran the 7th Marines 4.2-inch Mortar Company and interdicted the road between the 2nd and 3rd Battalions. By first light, they had succeeded in blocking the Main Supply Route (MSR), were in control of the area between the Marine rifle companies and the 2nd Battalion Command Post (CP). Sup-

port fire had to be called in quickly otherwise the Marines would have been annihilated. However, mortars, artillery and aircraft hit the enemy from all sides and hundreds of Chinese were slaughtered in the valley. By 1000 hours the 1st Battalion had secured the valley. The Chinese had lost over 662 men killed in the valley alone. The Chinese Regiments were badly mauled, and withdrew three miles from Sudong to a line set up by the 372nd Regiment. Litzenberg continued to advance north with his Marines. Taking Sudong, they moved on toward Chinhung-ni, a further six miles up the road. After eliminating four T-34 North Korean tanks which were hidden near Samgo Station, the 7th Marines settled into defensive positions around Chinhung-ni.

The Chinese held Funchilin Pass up ahead, and unknown to the Marines, they were nearing the enemy's forward line. Litzenberg dispatched the Recon Company to take the tip of Hill 891 (later called How Hill) as it commanded the road. The two advance jeeps were destroyed as soon as they turned the curve onto the main road and the 3rd Platoon got pinned down for 45 minutes before darkness set in

and allowed them to withdraw. The next day witnessed the Marines' attempt to take How Hill and Hill 897 but each attempt was beaten off by a very determined enemy. On 6 November the Marines charged up How Hill four times before they succeeded in taking the nose. The Chinese still held the crest but due to their ammunition running low the Marines were ordered to withdraw once again. The next morning they occupied How Hill as the enemy had retreated in the night. The Marines also occupied Hills 891 and 987. Casualties were starting to rise; the 7th Marines had 46 killed, 262 wounded and 6 missing in action. The Chinese were pulling back in front of the Marines, and on 10 November the 1st Battalion occupied Koto-ri. It was

Left: *A Marine who fought to keep the Communists out of Seoul symbolically tears up a picture of Stalin.*
Below: *Marine artillerymen bravely try to retaliate during intense fighting west of Seoul.*

the 175th anniversary of the Marine Corps. Winter struck that day, gale force winds and below zero temperatures, giving the Marines a preview of the suffering which was to come.

With direct engagement with the enemy temporarily stopped, the Marines went back to patrolling. On 11 November the X Corps ordered an advance to the border: the 1st Marines were on the left, I ROK Corps on the right, and the 7th Infantry Division in the center. The Marines were then ordered to change direction: instead of heading straight north, they were to move to Yudam-ni, then west to lessen the enormous gap between the X Corps and 8th Army. Major General Smith was worried about his left flank as he advanced. The 8th Army had already been pushed back in the west so the only thing the Chinese had to do was pivot across and his Marines would be in dire straits. Smith decided on his own initiative to strengthen the Hamhung-Hagaru road and garrison, the key points on the MSR. He ordered a slow advance and his caution paid off in the succeeding weeks. On 17 November the 5th Marines advanced along the east side of the Chosin Reservoir and were ordered to seize

168

Sinhung-ni, only some seven miles further than Hagaru. The Marines received some help from a previously unexpected source on the 21st – the 41st Independent Commando, Royal Marines, a unit of 235 reconnaissance men, commanded by Lieutenant Colonel Douglas Drysdale had specifically requested to work alongside its brother Marines. It was assigned to work with the Recon Company to protect the endangered left flank. The 21 November also witnessed the 17th Infantry, 7th Infantry Division reach the Yalu at Hyesanjin. This was the only American unit to actually get through to the border.

The day after Thanksgiving, the Marines were ordered to move out from Yudam-ni and move west and take Mupyong-ni, then continue to advance until they reached the Yalu.

This new plan would now expose both Marine flanks to attack. The Chinese did not take this new offensive sitting down. They defeated II ROK Corps, the right wing of the 8th Army, close to Tokchon, on 25 November. The next day saw the Chinese follow up by decimating the remaining units of II ROK Corps and roll back the 8th Army's offensive. Now the gap which Smith had been worried about widened to horrifying proportions. The Marines and the X Corps were not as yet under direct pressure from the Chinese armies but the Marines were freezing in 20-degree below zero weather. The severe cold froze everything in sight, including flesh, weapons, supplies and valuable equipment which at this stage could not be replaced. The Marines had drawn in their pickets to guard Yudam-ni, 3500 feet above sea level, and surrounded by five great ridges, on the crests of which waited the frozen 7th Marines. The night of 27 November, the Chinese commander General Lin Piao dispatched his finest field commander, General Sung Shin-lun, to force the X Corps into the sea and destroy the 1st Marine Division once and for all. In the following night's battle, the Marines fought a long and sustained attack for key positions and hills all along the ridges. By dawn the attacks had been beaten off, but the Marines were in bad shape. Litzenberg and Murray ordered the advance halted and for all Marine units to regroup. Smith then ordered the Marines to pull back and reopen the vital Hagaru road. The Marine counterattack had killed over 600 enemy and wounded another 500, but Marine casualties were more than 500.

Reinforcements were needed immediately from the south. At Koto-ri B Company, 31st Infantry and the 41st Commando, Royal Marines were organized into a small task force by Colonel Puller and ordered to fight their way 11 miles to Hagaru. Puller told Drysdale, the Royal Marine Commander, "They've got us surrounded . . . [but they] . . . won't get away this time."

Drysdale's men fought their way to within six miles of Hagaru before

Medal of honor winners – Korean War 1950-1953			
Name	*Location*	*Date*	*Unit*
Corporal Charles Abrell	Hill 1316	1951	1st Marines
Captain William Barber	Toktong Pass	1950	7th Marines
Private Hector Cafferata	Toktong Pass	1950	7th Marines
Private First Class William Baugh	Hell-Fire Valley	1950	1st Marines
Corporal David Champagne	Tumae-ri Ridge	1952	7th Marines
Private First Class Stanley Christianson	Seoul	1950	1st Marines
1st Lieutenant Henry Commiskey	Yongdungpo	1950	1st Marines
Corporal Jack Davenport	Songnae-Dong	1951	5th Marines
Lieutenant Colonel Raymond Davis	Toktong Pass	1950	7th Marines
Corporal Duane Dewey	Panmunjom	1952	5th Marines
Private First Class Fernando Garcia	Outpost Bruce	1952	5th Marines
Private First Class Edward Gomez	Hill 749	1951	1st Marines
Staff Sergeant Ambrosio Guillen	Hill 119	1953	7th Marines
Sergeant James Johnson	Yudam-ni	1950	11th Marines
Private First Class John Kelly	Tumae-ri Ridge	1952	7th Marines
Private First Class Jack Kelso	Outpost Warsaw	1952	7th Marines
Staff Sergeant Robert Kennemore	Yudam-ni	1950	7th Marines
Private First Class Herbert Littleton	Horseshoe Ridge	1951	7th Marines
1st Lieutenant Baldomero Lopez	Inchon	1950	5th Marines
Sergeant Daniel Matthews	Outpost Vegas	1953	7th Marines
Sergeant Frederick Mausert	Hill 673	1951	7th Marines
Private First Class Alford McLaughlin	Outpost Bruce	1952	5th Marines
1st Lieutenant Frank Mitchell	Hansan-ni	1950	7th Marines
Private First CLass Walter Monegan	Sosa-ri	1950	1st Marines
Private First Class Whitt Moreland	Yanggu	1951	5th Marines
2nd Lieutenant Raymond Murphy	Ungok Hill	1953	5th Marines
Major Reginald Meyers	Hagaru	1950	1st Marines
Private First Class Eugene Obregon	Seoul	1950	5th Marines
2nd Lieutenant George O'Brien	The Hook	1952	7th Marines
Corporal Lee Phillips	Sudong	1950	7th Marines
Sergeant James Poynter	Sudong	1950	7th Marines
2nd Lieutenant George Ramer	Hill 680	1951	7th Marines
2nd Lieutenant Robert Reem	Funchilin Pass	1950	7th Marines
Staff Sergeant William Shuck	Outpost Yoke	1952	7th Marines
Private First Class Robert Simanek	Outpost Irene	1952	5th Marines
Captain Carl Sitter	Hagaru	1950	1st Marines
2nd Lieutenant Sherrod Skinner	The Hook	1952	11th Marines
Staff Sergeant Archie Van Winkle	Sudong	1950	7th Marines
Corporal Joseph Vittori	Hill 749	1951	1st Marines
Staff Sergeant Lewis Watkins	Outpost Frisco	1952	7th Marines
Staff Sergeant Harold Wilson	Horseshoe Ridge	1951	1st Marines
Staff Sergeant William Windrich	Yudam-ni	1950	5th Marines

Total: 42

stopping due to night setting in. The valley where he halted became known as Hell-Fire Valley. It would go down in Marine Corps history as its ugliest defeat. The Chinese ambush caught the Marines between mortar and machine-gun fire from two sides. The entire advance section of some 400 men, consisting of 75 percent of the Royal Marines, the lead tanks, G Company and a few Army infantry, managed to fight their way to Hagaru and safety. The remainder of the men were cut to pieces although under Lieutenant Colonel Arthur Chidester they attempted to make a break for Koto-ri. What was left of this group under Major McLaughlin were forced to surrender or be annihilated with absolutely no hope for the wounded.

Marine privates Frank Albert, Hugh McKenna and Dennis Hogan await the signal to move. Note the amphibious trucks and tanks in the background.

Task Force Drysdale had lost 162 killed or missing and 159 wounded; of the force dispatched to break through to Koto-ri, only 300 men made it. MacArthur reported that he was now on the defensive against overwhelming enemy forces. The great gamble had failed. The Navy regathered its task force after sailing for friendly waters in the expectation of the war's immediate end, and rushed back to evacuate the beleaguered troops. The 1st Marine Aircraft Wing flew in five squadrons to Yonpo Field to cover the retreat. On 30 November at the Hagaru Conference, Major General Almond ordered the entire withdrawal of the Marine Force, from Yudam-ni to the sea, 78 long gruelling miles.

The break out began on 1 December at 0800 hours when Taplett's 3rd Battalion, 5th Marines took the main force down the road; Davis' 1st Battalion, 7th Marines were to make a dashing rescue eight miles away to get

US Marine Corps helicopter units

(To July 1953)

Marine Helicopter Squadron 1 (HMX 1)
Commissioned 1 December 1947, at Quantico, Virginia
Commanding Officers:
Colonel Edward C Dyer 1 December 47–25 June 49
Lieutenant Colonel John F Carey 26 June 49–9 July 50
Colonel Keith B McCutcheon 10 July 50–20 November 51
Lieutenant Colonel John H King 21 November 51–24 January 52
Lieutenant Colonel George W Herring 25 January 52–23 June 52
Lieutenant Colonel Edward V Finn 24 June 52–31 July 53

Headquarters Marine Helicopter Transport Group 16 (MAG(HR)-16)
Commissioned 1 March 52, at Santa Ana, California
Commanding Officers:
Colonel Harold J Mitchener 1–23 March 52
Colonel William D Roberson 24 March 52–2 June 52
Colonel Harold J Mitchener 3 June 52–31 July 53

Marine Air Base Squadron 16 (MABS-16)
Commissioned 1 March 52, Santa Ana, California
Commanding Officers:
Major William L Gunness 1 March 52–30 June 52
Captain Donald H Foss 1–31 July 52
Major Perry P McRobert 1 August 52–30 June 53
Major George F Bauman 1 July 53–25 July 53
Lieutenant Colonel Robert R Ayres 26 July 53–31 July 53

Headquarters Squadron, Marine Helicopter Transport Group 16 (HEDRON MAG(HR)-16)
Commissioned 1 March 52 at Santa Ana, California
Commanding Officers:
Captain Paul L Robinson 1 March 52–31 May 52
Captain Raymond D Dallam 1 June 52–16 October 52
Major William L Gunness 17 October 52–13 June 53
Major John N Wester 14 June 53–27 July 53
Major Joseph L Freitas 28 July 53–31 July 53

Marine Aircraft Maintenance Squadron 16 (MAMS-16)
Commissioned 1 March 52 at Santa Ana, California
Commanding Officers:
Major Tillman E Bishop 1 March 52–16 May 52
Major Edwin E Shifflet 17 May 52–31 July 53

Marine Helicopter Transport Squadron 161 (HMR-161)
Commissioned 15 January 51 at Santa Ana, California
Commanding Officers:
Lieutenant Colonel George W Herring 15 January 51–18 December 51
Colonel Keith B McCutcheon 19 December 51–6 August 52
Lieutenant Colonel John F Carey 7 August 52–15 March 53
Colonel Owen A Chambers 16 March 53–31 July 53

Marine Helicopter Transport Squadron 162 (HMR-162)
Commissioned 30 June 51 at Santa Ana, California
Commanding Officers:
Colonel Harold Mitchener 30 June 51–29 February 52
Major George Linnemeier 1 March 52–31 July 52
Major Tillman Bishop 1 August 52–31 October 52
Lieutenant Colonel James Johnson 1 November 52–13 May 53
Lieutenant Colonel Wallace Slappey 14 May 53–27 July 53
Major Dwain Lengel 28 July 53–31 July 53

Marine Helicopter Transport Squadron 163 (HMR-163)
Commissioned 1 December 1951 at Santa Ana, California
Commanding Officers:
Colonel William Roberson 1 December 51–25 February 52
Major Lynn Midkiff 26 February 52–29 May 52
Major Gerald Graff 30 May 52–30 June 52
Major Homer Daniel 1 July 52–30 June 53
Major Victor Armstrong 1 July 53–31 July 53

Marine Air Base Squadron 36 (MABS-36)
Commissioned 2 June 52 at Santa Ana, California
Commanding Officers:
Captain Robert Allen 2 June 52–1 September 52
Major John Sinderholm 1 September 52–20 March 53
Captain James Dorough 21 March 53–9 April 53
Captain Floyd Wines 10 April 53–30 July 53
Major Earl Langston 31 July 53

Marine Aircraft Maintenance Squadron 36 (MAMS-36)
Commissioned 2 June 52 at Santa Ana, California
Commanding Officers:
Major M D Hill 2 June 52–29 September 52
Major James Sawyer 30 September 52–31 October 52
Major Albert Simmons 1 November 52–4 February 53
Major Andrew McVicars 5 February 53–23 July 53
Major Walter Scarborough 24 July 53–31 July 53

Marine Helicopter Transport Squadron 361 (HMR-361)
Commissioned 25 February 52 at Santa Ana, California
Commanding Officers:
Colonel William Roberson 25 February 52–23 March 52
Major John Mahon 24 March 52–1 June 52
Major Donald Osen 2 June 52–31 October 52
Major Charles Samis 1 November 52–31 July 53

Marine Helicopter Transport Squadron 362 (HMR-362)
Commissioned 30 April 52 at Santa Ana, California
Commanding Officers:
Major William Rozier 30 April 52–31 October 52
Major James Sawyer 1 November 52–26 January 53
Major Edward Lupton 27 January 53–3 March 53
Major Arthur Hellerude 4 March 53–31 July 53

out the last company holding Toktong Pass. The key to the entire operation was whether the 1st MAW could get their Corsairs into the air to provide close-in support. Despite six inches of heavy snowfall, the Corsairs were in the air. They wanted a piece of the action and were not going to let any Marines get caught by the enemy as they withdrew. Smith said the Marines were now "attacking in another direction." The Marines fought their way to Hagaru, suffering 1500 casualties, quite a fight considering that it was done in below zero weather. The main worry now for the Marine commanders was the evacuation of the wounded. A standard was set when Captain Eugene Hering, Division Surgeon, stated that to be evacuated, an individual had to be in worse shape than Lieutenant Commander Chester Lessenden, 5th Marines' surgeon. Lessenden had both feet frozen, could not walk and was in extreme pain but refused to be airlifted out. By 5 December 4312 men were flown out of Hagaru, and another 537

reinforcements flown in. The USAF offered to evacuate all the troops at Hagaru but Major General Smith refused. The correspondent wanted to know whether this was a "retreat or retirement." Smith stated since they were surrounded, there was no rear, consequently there could be no retreat. In the two days, 6–7 December, the 1st Marine Division in its withdrawal to Koto-ri had lost 103 killed, 506 wounded and 7 missing in action. But the Marines had managed to bring out 10,000 troops and over 1000 vehicles.

The road from Koto-ri to safety was open to attack after attack as the Marines progressed slowly but surely through the mountain passes and steep ravines. Without the support of the 1st MAF, USAF and Naval carrier pilots, the Marines could not have succeeded in their break out and they were the first to acknowledge their debt. The 1st Marine Division had successfully beaten seven highly trained Chinese Divisions while accomplishing the break out. The division's final tally was

75 more killed, 256 wounded and 16 missing in action.

At Hungnam, 105,000 combat troops, 91,000 refugees, and 17,500 vehicles had to be evacuated by sea. Lieutenant General Shepard was there to oversee the entire operation and to insure that his Marines were adequately provided for. By 14 December 22,215 Marines were on board transports and heading for Pusan. The Chosin Reservoir campaign was finally over. A new page was added to Marine Corps history.

The final epitaph for those gallant Marines who fought and died in the running fight from Hagaru to Hamhung was made by General MacArthur:

This was undoutedbly one of the most successful strategic retreats in history, comparable with and markedly similar to Wellington's great Peninsula withdrawal. Had the initiative action not been taken and an inert position of adequate defense

Marine Helicopter Transport Squadron 363 (HMR-363)
Commissioned 2 June 52 at Santa Ana, California
Commanding Officers:
Major Andrew McVicars 2 June 52–31 October 52
Major Dwain Lengel 1 November 52–13 March 53
Lieutenant Colonel Robert Ayres Jr 14 March 53–26 April 53
Major Dwain Lengel 27 April 53–24 July 53
Major Jesse Morrison 25 July 53–30 July 53
Major John Doherty 31 July 53

Marine Observation Squadron 1 (VMO-1)
Received Helicopters in September 1951 and was attached to the 2nd Marine Division
Commanding Officers:
Lieutenant Colonel Robert Teller 15 July 49–29 December 51
Lieutenant Colonel George Hollowell 31 December 51–31 July 53

Marine Observation Squadron 2 (VMO-2)
Received Helicopters in July 1951 and was attached to the 3rd Marine Division   Commanding Officers:
Lieutenant Colonel William Abblitt 15 June 51–31 October 52
Major William MacLean 1 November 52–31 July 53

Marine Observation Squadron 6 (VMO-6)
Received Helicopters in July 1950 and was attached to the 1st Marine Division   Commanding Officers:
Major Vincent Gottschalk 3 July 50–4 April 51
Major David McFarland 5 April 51–30 September 51
Major Kenneth Smedley 1 October 51–31 October 51
Major Edward Polgrean 1 November 51–30 January 52
Major Kenneth Smedley 1 February 52–10 February 52
Major William MacLean Jr 11 February 52–26 February 52
Lieutenant Colonel William Herring 27 February 52–9 May 52
Major Wallace Slappey Jr 10 May 52–9 September 52
Lieutenant Colonel Elkins Dew 10 September 52–1 February 53
Lieutenant Colonel William Cloman 2 February 53–30 June 53
Lieutenant Colonel Earl Anderson 1–31 July 53

Headquarters Marine Helicopter Transport Group 26 (MAG(HR)-26)
Commissioned 16 June 52 at Cherry Point, North Carolina
Commanding Officers:
Colonel Owen Chambers 16 June 52–28 July 52
Lieutenant Colonel Frank Collins 29 July 52–4 January 53
Colonel Martin Severson 6 January 53–30 March 53
Lieutenant Colonel Frank Collins 31 March 53–31 July 53

Headquarters Squadron, Marine Helicopter Transport Group 26 (HEDRON, MAG(HR)-26)
Commissioned 16 June 52 at Cherry Point, North Carolina
Commanding Officers:
Captain William Hosch 16 June 52–16 November 52
Captain Wallace Wessel 17 November 52–9 April 53
Captain Marion Daane 10 April 53–31 July 53

Marine Air Base Squadron 26 (MABS-26)
Commissioned 16 June 52 at Cherry Point, North Carolina
Commanding Officers:
Captain William Smiley 16–27 June 52
Major Virgil Olson 28 June 52–31 July 52
Major William Eldridge 1–21 August 52
Major Roy Dasher 22 August 52–24 February 53
Major Ray Lemmons 25 February 53–2 March 53
Lieutenant Colonel Vernon Ullman 3 March 53–31 July 53

Marine Aircraft Maintenance Squadron 26 (MAMS-26)
Commissioned 16 June 52 at Cherry Point, North Carolina
Commanding Officer:
Major James Cotton 16 June 52–31 July 53

Marine Helicopter Transport Squadron 261 (HMR-261)
Commissioned 5 April 51 at Cherry Point, North Carolina
Lieutenant Colonel Owen Chambers 5 April 51–15 June 52
Major Stanley Titterud 16 June 52–24 February 53
Major Roy Dasher 25 February 53–31 July 53

Marine Helicopter Transport Squadron 262 (HMR-262)
Commissioned 1 September 51 at Cherry Point, North Carolina
Commanding Officers:
Lieutenant Colonel William Doolen 1 September 51–20 January 52
Lieutenant Colonel David Danser 21 January 52–27 March 52
Lieutenant Colonel Frank Hopper 28 March 52–9 September 52
Major Robert Rathbun 10 September 52–31 July 53

Marine Helicopter Transport Squadron 263 (HMR-263)
Commissioned 16 June 52 at Cherry Point, North Carolina
Commanding Officers:
Major William Crapo 16 June 52–14 June 53
Lieutenant Colonel John Newlands 15 June 53–31 July 53

Headquarters Marine Helicopter Transport Group 36 (MAG(HR)-36)
Commissioned 2 June 52 at Santa Ana, California
Commanding Officers:
Colonel William Roberson 2 June 52–15 January 53
Lieutenant Colonel Charles Prall 16 January 53–June 53
Major John Sinderholm 12 June 53–27 July 53
Lieutenant Colonel Wallace Slappey 28 July 53–31 July 53

Headquarters Squadron Marine Helicopter Transport Group 36 (HEDRON, MAG(HR)-36)
Commissioned 2 June 52 at Santa Ana, California
Commanding Officers:
Captain James Bruce 2–4 June 52
Captain Rodney Montgomery 4 June 52–17 July 52
Captain Kerwin Jacobs 18 July 52–31 July 52
Major Herbert Lewis 1 August 52–19 September 52
Captain John Magouyrk, Jr 20 September 52–29 September 52
Major Dwain Lengel 30 September 52–31 October 52
Major Samuel Sampler 1 November 52–9 Feb 53
Captain John Magouyrk 10 February 53–31 July 53

---

assumed, I have no slightest doubt that the Eighth Army and the X Corps would have been annihilated.

The Marines were back at Masan and were recuperating. On 23 December Lieutenant General Walton Walker, 8th Army commander, was killed in a road accident. The man selected to replace Walker was not unknown to the Marines – Lieutenant General Matthew Ridgway, the great paratroop leader. The Chinese now had the advantage, and quickly pressed it home. They took Seoul, Inchon and Wonju again and decimated the 2nd US and 8th ROK Divisions in the process. Ridgway launched a counter-offensive and the Marines were once again in the thick of the fighting. Non-stop fighting continued through April 1951. On 11 April Truman fired General MacArthur. This happened as a result of a long and hot contest of wills, and gross insubordination on the part of MacArthur to his Commander in Chief. Politics were involved and

Truman really had no other choice but to fire MacArthur. Ridgway took over the UN Command and Lieutenant General James Van Fleet assumed command of the 8th Army. By 25 June 1951 the US was ready to accept the *status quo ante*, and make peace along the 38th Parallel. The Korean War was now one-year-old and in that time 1,250,000 men had been killed, wounded or missing in action. As for the civilians as usual they suffered most, over two million dead and a further three million homeless. For another two years the fighting went on, with feelers being put out by both sides to see if there was any advantage which could be gained. Finally after three years, one month and a couple of days, the Armistice was signed. The Marines lost 4262 killed and 20,038 wounded in action. Wars of containment on the Asian continent were costly, yet this was but a prelude to the longest war in US history, which would start in less than a decade and on the same continent.

Platoon 285 Drill instructor Sergeant Warren Plavets marches his platoon off the drill fields after graduation in 1952.

Phnom Penh in April 1975, seen from the left gunner port of a Sikorsky CH-53 helicopter as it comes in to make a landing on a soccer field near the river. The helicopter based at Kaneohe, Hawaii, was attached to the USS Hancock.

The Green Berets

Between Korea and Vietnam the United States Marines were involved in two major operations.

Lebanon

The first of these major actions occurred in 1958 when the President of Lebanon, Camille Chamoun, requested US help in restoring some form of peace to his politically unstable and riot-racked country. The decision was made at the highest level to intervene in Lebanon's internal affairs by President Dwight D Eisenhower. The political situation in the Middle East at the time was the root cause behind the unrest in Lebanon. When Gamal Nasser became President of Egypt in 1954, the Arab world was split right down the middle. Nasser made an immediate arms deal with the Soviets, and Syria followed in his footsteps. Iraq and Jordan decided after much deliberation to go with the Western powers. In July 1956 Nasser nationalized the Suez Canal – Israel, France and Britain fielded an expeditionary force to retake the canal, but the US and the UN put a halt to this. Lebanon attempted to play the part of the neutral, its population was divided between the Christian faith and Moslem religion. The situation was about to ignite like a powder keg. Chamoun's problems took on international importance when on 14 July, a military coup overthrew the pro-Western government in Iraq and executed the king. Hussein of Jordan was also in mortal danger of being assassinated. Western domination in the Middle East was endangered. With this potential crisis in the making, Eisenhower ordered General Nathan Twining, Chairman of the Joint Chiefs of Staff, to land amphibious units of the 6th Fleet in Lebanon. This order caught the Fleet Marines, under Brigadier General Sydney Wade, off balance so that his forces were split and of three Battalions, only one of the 2nd Battalion, 2nd Marines, under Lieutenant Colonel Harry Hadd could be ready in 24 hours to make the landing. The 1st Battalion, 8th Marines was on its way home. The 3rd Battalion, 6th Marines was relieving the 1st Battalion which was *en route* from Crete to Athens. The only thing that saved the day was the fact that the LSD *Fort Snelling* which had been supporting the 3rd Battalion, 6th Marines was off Rhodes and only 400 miles from Lebanon.

On 15 July Admiral Burke, Chief of Naval Operations, advised Admiral James Holloway in London and Vice-Admiral Brown, Commander of the 6th Fleet, of the President's decision to dispatch Marines to Beirut by 1500 hours local time to take the International Airport. At Red Beach, at 1504 hours, the Marines were landing and in a few minutes were in control of the airport. There was no opposition but then none had been expected. The commander of the Lebanese Army was General Fuad Chehab who was worried that the army would split into factions if the situation did not improve. The Lebanon crisis resulted from political and military confusion.

The US Ambassador, Robert McClintock, and US Naval officers as well as Lieutenant Colonel Hadd could not achieve any form of co-ordination at all. The whole operation produced much bad feeling between the State Department and the military.

The next day the 3rd Battalion, 6th Marines landed and Wade ordered Hadd's battalion to advance on Beirut. McClintock and Chehab requested that the Marines not attempt to enter the capital because the Lebanese Army might decide to stop them. The Ambassador asked Wade to stop the battalion but Wade refused. President Chamoun then conferred with Wade and McClintock and subsequently agreed to allow the Marines to enter the city. Now a confrontation was in the making because the Lebanese Army had moved units up on the main road and was blocking it with tanks. Chehab asked for a delay and Wade gave him another 30 minutes. At 1100 hours the Marines advanced on Beirut until they stopped directly in front of the Lebanese Army units which had blocked the road, a mile from the airport. The Lebanese meant business and had their weapons pointing at the Marines' leading vehicles. This potential crisis was avoided when the column started again led by the Ambassador's car and by-passed all rebel strongpoints in the city. Lebanese Army co-operation with the Marines increased as the days went by. On 29 September, the 3rd Battalion, 6th Marines departed from the Lebanon leaving a small US Army contingent to take their place. By 23 October a more balanced

An HR2S-1 photographed in 1957.

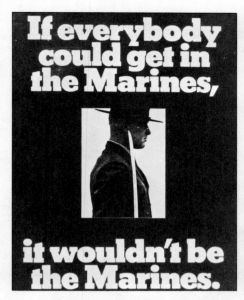

If everybody could get in the Marines, it wouldn't be the Marines.

The Marines are looking for a few good men to join them.

"Wear this Proudly"... U·S·MARINES

government was established with members from both majority parties taking an active part. On 25 October with their peace-keeping role concluded the last US troops pulled out of Lebanon.

The Dominican Republic

The next international crisis which involved the use of United States Marines was back in their old stomping grounds, the Caribbean. The Marines landed in the Dominican Republic on 28 April 1965. President Johnson was determined that his term in office would not be clouded by another Cuba

being born in the Caribbean. One Castro was enough. The US had itself encouraged direct elections in the Dominican Republic after the ouster of President Joaquin Balaguer. His successor was a very popular citizen, Juan Bosch. He was only in office seven months when a military coup, backed by conservative interests sent him to exile in Puerto Rico. The US recognized the new regime but only on the condition that they hold elections by 1965. The new government was headed by Reid Cabral, and was extremely unpopular. On 24 April 1965 the Dominican Army revolted and demanded the return of Bosch to office. Pro-Bosch troops took up positions throughout Santo Domingo and his sympathizers handed out weapons to the crowds. Cabral re-

quested that the US intervene as the situation was beyond his control.

Cabral was arrested soon after and forced to resign. Meanwhile the Caribbean Ready Group was steaming toward the Dominican Republic just in case it became necessary to evacuate US citizens. This group had aboard the 3rd Battalion, 6th Marines, a Marine Helicopter Squadron, and 1702 Marines of the 6th Marine Expeditionary Unit. The anti-Bosch leader, General Elias Wessin y Wessin requested that US troops intervene to stop the fighting. Diplomatically it was impossible for the US to support an unpopular regime against the people's choice. The Embassy was ordered to stay neutral, attempt to get a ceasefire and prepare to evacuate American citizens. On that Tuesday, the ugliest

battle in Dominican history took place in the streets of the capital where hundreds of people were killed. The evacuation went ahead, and by Tuesday evening the crisis appeared to be over, with the anti-Bosch forces winning. This was a short-lived victory. They failed to follow up their initial success and the pro-Bosch forces marshalled and drove the anti-Bosch troops out of the city. On Wednesday Colonel Pedro Benoit, the leader of a new anti-Bosch party, requested that the Marines be put ashore. Now there was no hesitation; Marines landed on the embassy ground by helicopter and immediately returned pro-Bosch fire. By 1800 hours a further 500 Marines had landed from the helicopter carrier, *Boxer*. The political situation was now clearly out of control. Fighting became increasingly heavy in the city. Mediation was called for and President Johnson dispatched former Ambassador John B Martin to act as his personal representative. Before the International Security Zone was established and the Inter-American Peace Force created, the US ground strength in the Dominican Republic stood at 22,200 men with an additional 10,000 standing by offshore. The Marines were withdrawn by 6 June, after the first contingent of Brazilian troops had arrived. The Dominicans elected Balaguer president on 1 June 1966. By the end of the summer all remaining US troops were withdrawn. Thus ended another page in the history of the Marine Corps. American foreign policy took another hammering from critics on its totally illegal intervention in the internal affairs of a small nation.

US Policy in Southeast Asia

The global significance of Vietnam and Indo-China is a phenomenon of recent history. This area of the world has made few important contributions to the West, or for that matter, to the East. In the earlier trading days, it held some importance to mariners as a station for trade between China, India and the rest of Southeast Asia. This disappeared with the development of accurate compasses and large seagoing ships. The country had virtually nothing to export, and Western traders who had business interests there made little or no profit from their trade. The stakes of the war in Vietnam were far greater than the economic assets, population or territorial gains. The total US investment and trading interests in all of Southeast Asia were inconsequential when compared to

similar interests in Europe and Latin America. The loss of all Southeast Asia's rubber, tin and other miscellaneous products indigenous to that part of the world would not noticeably affect the US economy. As for economic benefits, the US could expect none in this area in the foreseeable future to justify the tremendous expenditure of American money and manpower in Vietnam. Of course, it can be argued that the US was not fighting in Vietnam for any economic gain, but for the rights of small nations to be free of aggression and have the right of self-determination. Therefore Vietnam was a testing ground of ideologies and wills between the Communist and non-Communist states.

President Eisenhower summed up the importance of Vietnam in 1959 when he referred to the "domino theory." This misapplied misnomer implied that Asian countries had no more self-determination than a row of dominoes. He stated:

Strategically, South Vietnam's capture by the Communists would bring their power several hundred miles into a hitherto free region. The remaining countries of Southeast Asia would be menaced by a great flanking movement. . . . The loss of South Vietnam would set into motion a crumbling process that could as it progressed have grave consequences for us and for freedom.

Diplomats argued that a Communist conquest of Southeast Asia would divide the world in two. India and Pakistan would be flanked, Australia and New Zealand in real danger of being cut off from the rest of the world. The US declared that it did not want a major confrontation with the Communist powers. Officially US policy in Vietnam desired an independent South Vietnam whose people were free to choose their own government (as long as it was not Communist) without fear of interference from any outside source, an end to the covert and overt fighting, and to show that it stood by its commitments not to allow these so-called "wars of liberation" backed by the Communist powers to succeed. This is the political background with which the US Marine Corps had to contend when they arrived in South Vietnam. They were deployed to protect the rights and independence of a sovereign nation which did not have the ability to do so itself.

Left: *ARVN men quickly unload supplies in a jungle clearing (1964).*
Below left: *Men of 7th Marines.*
Below: *An A-4D Sky Ranger.*

Vietnam

The "leatherneck" in Vietnam was quite a man. The feeling was that most back-homers, including Congress, did not understand or accept the very real truth that the conflict in Vietnam was a war. The bulk of Americans consider Southeast Asia with nothing but confusion and contempt. A Marine returning home from a stint in Vietnam in late 1967 would find that people did not even know where that country was on the map, and could not guess at the number of weekly casualties there, who the enemy was and what was being contested. Vietnam! Brother, you should have been in New York during the blackout. Or, Da Nang? You should have been at the Battle of the Bulge now that was a real fight. Americans did not know, did not care and could not be bothered by a war they just could not identify with. Vietnam was too far away.

In the "leatherneck's" world there was a nightly blackout followed by heavy mortar and artillery fire and constant search-and-destroy missions.

It was alive with booby traps and occupied by an enemy and an ally who looked exactly the same. He would have given a month's pay for just one night's sound sleep. The primary point was that the average age of a "leatherneck" in Vietnam was 19. The pink-cheeked, tousle-haired, tight-muscled, unmarried, young man was the backbone of US combat ground strength in Vietnam and he carried on the proud traditions of the Corps. In all the years of US involvement in Vietnam, the US Marine Corps was never defeated in battle.

What most people do not know is that this was not the first time United States Marines had landed in Vietnam but the second. The first was in 1853 when Marines from the USS *Constitution* landed in what is now the city of Da Nang in I Corps. They landed the first time to serve the US's interests in the Far East. They landed the second time for the same reason.

The Marine air-ground team in Vietnam was known as the III Marine Amphibious Force (III MAF) and was composed of the 1st and 3rd Marine Divisions, the 1st Marine Aircraft Wing, Force Logistics Command and various supporting elements. Together with Vietnamese forces, other US Forces and Free World Military Forces, the III Marine Amphibious Force blunted every enemy threat in the five northernmost provinces.

Members of the III MAF had the distinction of being part of the largest field US Marine command that the USA has ever deployed on the field of battle. To quote General William Westmoreland, former Commander US Military Assistance Command in Vietnam (MACV), "Its military feats will go down in history."

The Presidential Unit Citation (PUC) was awarded to the 26th Marine Regiment and its reinforcing units held the Khe Sanh combat complex during the massive seven-week attack by two North Vietnamese divisions and exacted a bloody toll from the enemy while keeping his large force tied down. The 5th Marine Regiment also received the Presidential Unit Citation for Operations Union and Union II in which it totally decimated the 2nd North Vietnamese Army (NVA) Division and eliminated it as an effective fighting force for over four months. The Marine air-ground concept pioneered by the Corps in the 1930s, proved itself in Vietnam time and time again. Recognition was given both to the 1st Marine Division and the 1st Marine Aircraft Wing when they received the Presidential Unit Citation during October 1968 by the then Secretary of the Navy, Paul Ignatius. The 3rd Marine Division had already received the Presidential Unit Citation in 1967. With the arrival of adequate troops to I Corps, Marines were able to put the air-ground concept to its fullest use. Utilizing helicopter-borne assaults, another innovation pioneered by the Corps in the 1950s, the 3rd Marine Division maintained a mobile posture which had kept the enemy completely off-guard, never knowing where the Marines would strike next.

From 1954 to 1962 Marines were limited to advisory duties with the Vietnamese Marine Corps. This role changed drastically in April 1962, when a helicopter squadron was sent to Soc Trang, in the Mekong Delta to help train and support the Vietnamese Air Force and to provide logistical support for the Vietnamese Armed Forces. Three years later, the 9th Marine Expeditionary Brigade landed at Da Nang in I Corps, on 8 March 1965, the first US ground force to arrive in the country. From that time until 1972 Marines expanded their control from 249 square miles to 2000 square miles, killing over 90,800 of the enemy in the process.

On 8 March 1965 the 3rd Battalion, 9th Marines hit the beach just north of Da Nang in I Corps. They were greeted by laughing Vietnamese whores who draped the Marines with garlands of multi-colored tropical flowers. These troops were the first US troops to be committed to the Vietnam war. The I Company, 9th Marines took Hill 327 and K Company, Hill 268 just to the north. Meanwhile the 3rd Marines were assigned to guard the airfield and defend the base against enemy infiltrators. Everything surrounding the base from across the Cau Do River to within a mile south of the base, was Viet Cong territory. I Corps Tactical Zone (TZ) was the northernmost military region of South Vietnam, and it stretched from the 17th parallel, down to the southernmost spur of the Annamite Mountain Range at Sa Huynh. Within this tactical zone lived over 2,700,000 people of various ethnic groups, religious beliefs and political ideals. South Vietnamese troops held the large towns like Da Nang, but the Viet Cong (VC) held the countryside and were supported to a large extent by the common people. It was from these Vietnamese who wanted to be left alone that the VC received the majority of their support. These people did not

Right: *Vietnam at the time of the Tet Offensive.*
Below: *Marines take part in Operation Cormorant, a search and destroy mission conducted north of Da Nang.*

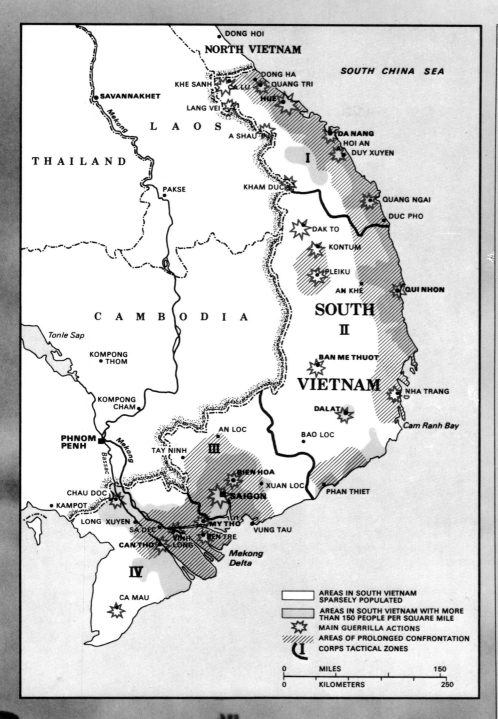

I Corps
(Total Population: 2,902,334)

Provinces	Chief Towns	Province Population
Quang Tri	Quang Tri	279,088
Thua Thien	Hue & Da Nang	633,799
Quang Nam	Hoi An	915,123
Quang Tin	Tam Ky	306,518
Quang Ngai	Quang Ngai	678,806

II Corps
(Total Population: 2,888,589)

Provinces	Chief Towns	Province Population
Binh Dinh	Qui Nhon	902,085
Binh Thuan	Phan Thiet	267,306
Darlac	Ban Me Thuot	293,194
Khanh Hoa	Nha Trang	403,988
Kontum	Kontum	104,241
Lam Dong	Bao Loc	65,651
Ninh Thuan	Phan Rang	156,194
Phu Ban	Hau Ban	51,313
Phu Yen	Tuy Hoa	329,464
Pleiku	Pleiku	192,682
Quang Duc	Gia Nghia	28,863
Tuyen Duc	Dalat	93,646

III Corps
(Total Population: 4,692,623)

Provinces	Chief Town	Province Population
Bien Hoa	Bien Hoa	449,468
Binh Duong	Phu Cuong	235,404
Binh Long	An Loc	70,394
Binh Tuy	Ham Tan	59,082
Hau Nghia	Khiem Cuong	224,118
Long An	Tan An	334,566
Long Khanh	Xuan Loc	144,227
Phuoc Long	Phuoc Le	104,213
Tay Ninh	Tay Ninh	235,404

IV Corps
(Total Population: 5,714,661)

Provinces	Chief Town	Province Population
An Giang	Long Xuyen	491,710
An Xuyen	Quan Long	235,398
Ba Xuyen	Khanh Hung	352,971
Bac Lieu	Vinh Loi	259,891
Chau Doc	Chau Phu	575,916
Choung Thien	Vi Thanh	248,713
Dinh Tuong	My Tho	547,899
Go Cong	Go Cong	173,748
Kien Giang	Rach Gia	387,634
Kien Hoa	Truc Giang	582,099
Kien Phong	Cao Lanh	320,478
Kien Tuong	Moa Hoa	42,597
Phong Dinh	Can Tho	426,090
Sa Dec	Sa Dec	264,511
Vinh Binh	Phu Vinh	404,118
Vinh Long	Vinh Long	500,870
Capital Military District		
Gia Dinh	Gia Dinh	1,089,773
Saigon	Saigon	1,622,673

A MacDonnell F4-B Phantom II. This was a carrier-borne, all-weather fighter and striker aircraft.

understand the politics behind the war; they only wanted to grow their crops to have sufficient food to feed their families.

On 10 April 1965 Lieutenant Colonel David Clement's 2nd Battalion, 3rd Marines arrived reinforcing the Marines at Da Nang. Also arriving on the 10 April was VMFA-531, composed of F4B Phantom jets, to give the Marine ground combat force adequate air cover whenever it was required. The Marine build up continued and on

7 May, Brigadier General Marion Carl landed a 6000-man brigade at Chu Lai, some 57 miles south of Da Nang. Lieutenant General Krulak, Fleet Marine Commander, wanted a second tactical jet strip to be built here at Chu Lai. The airfield was one of the new Short Airfield for Tactical Support (SATS) with aluminum runway matting, arresting gear and catapults. By 1 June the runway was completed and Douglas A-4 Skyhawks were starting to land. The Viet Cong started initiating attacks against friendly forces throughout May and June, so that by the first week in June, US Marine casualties were 179 wounded

and 29 killed in action. The scope of the war was now changing rapidly, the Marines were no longer committed to fighting as advisers to the South Vietnamese and securing coastal facilities. In the words of former Marine Corps Commandant, Wallace Green, Marines were in Vietnam to "kill Viet Cong."

Throughout the remainder of the year American commitments on the ground were increasing rapidly. With this combat commitment came an increase in Marine Corps strength which was raised from 193,000 to 223,000 men. During the month of July the Defense Department with authorization of the President sent the 1st Air Cavalry Division to Vietnam, bringing the total US ground strength to 125,000 men. The main policy-making decision of that time, which was later to rebound upon the in-house administration, was not to call up the reserves. To compensate for this action, the draft was doubled and voluntary enlistments stepped up. But the decision to increase draft totals intensified public opinion against the ground war in Vietnam. The Marines had four regiments and four air groups in Vietnam by mid-August. August was not a good month for the Marines because on the 3rd they were involved in their first serious and controversial

Marines of E Company, 1st Marine Division move across rice paddies under heavy fire southeast of Da Nang.

atrocity of the war. CBS reporter, Morley Safer witnessed US Marines of the 1st Battalion, 9th Marines burn down all of the dwellings in the village of Cam Ne, southwest of Da Nang.

On 18 August the Marines launched their first offensive, Operation Starlite. Colonel Oscar Peatross, commanded three battalions in a move against the 1st Viet Cong Regiment on the Van Tuong Peninsula, approximately 15 miles from Chu Lai. On that day two Marines earned the Medal of Honor for heroic action while engaged with superior enemy forces. The first was Corporal Robert O'Malley, I Company, 3rd Marines, who led his squad against a firmly entrenched enemy position. O'Malley ran across an adjacent rice paddy, threw himself unaided into the enemy trench and single-handedly wiped out eight Viet Cong with rifle fire and grenades. The second was Corporal Joe Paul, H Company, 4th Marines who near Nam Yen, placed himself directly in front of five wounded Marines who were being attacked by a superior enemy force. He succeeded in covering the wounded men until they could be evacuated but he was severely wounded and later died.

Operation Starlite ended when the Marines eliminated the Viet Cong force which had dug in with their backs to the sea, resulting in over 614 VC killed. The Marines continued operations along the coast, joined in combined operations with the South Vietnamese Marines and even initiated a pacification program. By December 1965 Marines casualties were on the rise: 454 dead and 2093 wounded since the Da Nang landings.

By mid-1966 there were 180,000 American troops in Vietnam, including 38,000 Marines. On the political front President Johnson called a halt to the bombing of North Vietnam, and once again attempted to initiate peace talks. Meanwhile, the 1st Marine Division's remaining units were deployed to Vietnam to occupy the provinces of Quang Tin and Quang Nai, the two southernmost provinces of I Corps. February and March saw the Marines engaged in intense heavy fighting. On 27 February the 2nd Battalion, 1st Marines rescued an ARVN regiment northeast of Phu Bai and assaulted well-entrenched Viet Cong positions to the north. Throughout 4, 5 and 6 March, Marine units were engaged in fire fights all around the city of Quang Ngai; when the action was completed it was estimated that one-third of the 36th NVA regiment had been decimated. The main action of the month was on the night of 9 March, when the Special Forces' forward camp at A Shau was wiped out in a heavy two-day

fight. Air Force and Marine aircraft flew close-in ground support for the outgunned, outnumbered and besieged defenders. The camp could not be succored, and on 11 March an evacuation was initiated. During this intense fighting the Marines lost three helicopters and one A-4C, which shows the intensity of the enemy fire on the supporting forces. Of the original force garrisoning the camp, 12 out of 17 Green Berets and 172 men of the Vietnamese garrison of 400 were finally evacuated. The war was definitely escalating for the Marines. The 1st Marine Division was now commanded by Major General Lewis Fields and was headquartered at Chu Lai. Lieutenant General Walt was commander of the III MAF and the 3rd Marine Division was under Major General Wood Kyle.

The next action of note and one of the most outstanding of the entire war occurred 25 miles went of Chu Lai. The 1st Platoon, C Company, 1st Reconnaissance Battalion, under Staff

Aviation Ordnance men position special weapons on a McDonnell Douglas A-4D Skyhawk.

Sergeant Jimmie Howard was ordered to hold an observation post on Hill 488. On the third night, at 2200 hours on 15 June, Howard's 18-men platoon on Hill 488 was attacked by a North Vietnamese battalion. Corporal Ricardo Binns had four men at an advance position when the enemy struck. Binns was hit immediately but shot and killed one enemy soldier and ordered each Marine to throw a grenade and withdraw back to the crest. Only two made it back; the rest died fighting the enemy in hand-to-hand combat. The remaining Marines under Staff Sergeant Howard's direction dug in and threw back each and every concentrated enemy assault. Howard was severly wounded in the legs by a

Four Vought F-8D Crusader in flight over California. They were standard US Navy carrier-borne jet fighters.

A Marine observation plane makes a low-level pass over Hue during the Tet Offensive in 1968.

grenade but, undaunted, passed his ammunition to the other men and called for artillery and air support. The North Vietnamese screamed: "Marines, you die!" Flares revealed an enemy horde waiting to overrun the small Marine post. The Marines had exhausted their supply of hand grenades, and resorted to firing single shots at the enemy and throwing rocks. When the sun rose over Hill 488, five Marines were dead and every other man was wounded, but they had held out. Evacuation helicopters were making their approach but Howard, as cool as ever, waved them off and called for additional strikes to secure the landing zone. The first helicopter was commanded by Major William Goodsell; it was hit immediately and Goodsell died from his wounds. A second helicopter was also hit. Finally, additional helicopters landed 1st Lieutenant Marshall Darling's C Company, 5th Marines onto the southern slope. C Company advanced up the hill and eliminated all enemy

The US and South Vietnamese bombed the Citadel of Hue during Tet to break the Viet Cong stranglehold.

resistance as it went. Howard's Marines only had eight rounds of ammunition left. The fighting continued but by the end of the day the enemy was beaten and knew it. Howard received the Medal of Honor for saving his platoon from certain destruction. Binns and Corpsman Billie Holmes were awarded the Navy Cross.

The war escalated with Marine Corps strength reaching 278,184 men by 1 July 1967, higher than its Korean War peak strength. Now with elements of the 5th Marine Division, the 26th, 27th and 28th Marines, and the 13th Marines utilized as artillery deployed to Vietnam, Corps strength in-country was 60,000. So far they had killed over 7300 enemy in battle and themselves lost 1700 dead and 9000 wounded. The Marines were firm believers in "clear and hold" tactics while the US Army's policy was "search and destroy." The Marines continued to fight this political, psychological and nerve-shattering war in the only way they knew how. They fought through Quang Nam province, the Que Son Valley and the Khe Sanh plateau.

Khe Sanh is a name which must go down in the annals of the Corps as one of its most epic and gallant defenses. Khe Sanh was an Advance Combat Base with a small airstrip, located in the mountainous jungle of northwest

Vietnam. Throughout March and April, Marine units were absorbing heavy losses in the vicinity of Hill 861. On 25 April Colonel John Lanigan's 3rd Battalion, 3rd Marines were airlifted into Khe Sanh and engaged the enemy on Hill 861. The 2nd Battalion was also deployed to Khe Sanh and by 28 April the hill was in Marine hands.

Even further west the 2nd Battalion took Hill 881 North and the 3rd Battalion Hill 881 South but before these objectives were achieved the Marines had to call up massive artillery and air support from the 1st MAW. The Marines did not find the task of taking the hills easy because the NVA regiment holding them put up intense resistance. The NVA were pulling back though and major damage was inflicted on the 325C NVA Division. The 3rd Marines were relieved by the 26th Marines, and the first Battle of Khe Sanh was completed with 155 Marines killed and 425 wounded. This was only the beginning, much more was to come. The Marines were committed to Operations Union I and Union II in June and Operation Adair at the end of June.

Meanwhile the enemy was building up its forces near Khe Sanh again and sporadic fighting continued through the rest of June and July. The North Vietnamese stepped up artillery and mortar barrages against Marine positions at Dong Ha, Da Nang, Phu Bai and Marble Mountain, causing substantial damage to supplies, equipment and aircraft, as well as killing men, during August and September. At the end of the year, the Marines could say that they were involved in the heaviest fighting of the year and had still managed to keep a tight control over the northern area of South Vietnam. The close of 1967 saw 77,679 Marines in III MAF. There were 21 Marine Battalions, 15 US Army Battalions, 4 Korean Marine Battalions and 31 ARVN battalions in I Corps.

The year 1968 will always be remembered by the US Forces who served in the Republic of South Vietnam. General William Westmoreland, Commander of MACV, assumed that the enemy would begin a major offensive around Khe Sanh and moved troops northward to combat this threat. This was exactly what North Vietnamese General Vo Nguyen Giap (the great military leader of the Viet Minh who inflicted defeat upon the French at Dien Bien Phu) had planned – the movement of key American troops from the populated cities and towns. Behind the six-mile deep DMZ were waiting the crack NVA 324B and 325C Divisions. By 15 January 1968 the 304th NVA Division was on the move from Laos to join with the 325C near Khe Sanh. At the start of the year there were over a quarter of a million allied troops committed to I Corps. Of the Marine Corps' total strength of 298,498, 81,249 men were in I Corps alone. Westmoreland keyed his entire defensive structure around the Khe Sanh Base complex. He felt – and rightly so – that it was a huge plug in the western basin of the DMZ, and firmly believed that if it fell to the enemy, the Marine Defenses along the DMZ would be flanked. Khe Sanh was reinforced so that it would not become an American Dien Bien Phu. This controversial decision was objective in nature, and a rational one in the restricted sense, and if followed

through accurately could be called an analytic paradigm. The height to which this decision-making policy was carried out went as far as the President himself. The Joint Chiefs of Staff gave their approval in writing. Yet the US Ambassador to South Vietnam and a retired Chairman of the Joint Chiefs of Staff, Maxwell Taylor, disagreed vehemently. Here again we deal with the integration of values and the handling of uncertainty by the actual decision-makers. The decision to hold Khe Sanh was such an example. In the words of an Air Force historian, "The base had become a symbol of US determination to see the war through." The actual responsibility for holding Khe Sanh was in the hands of Colonel David Lownds' 26th Marines. Four enemy regiments were sighted within 20 kilometers of the airstrip. The 2nd and 3rd Battalions of the 26th Marines were shifted from the coast to help the 1st Battalion in its defensive position. The scene was now set for the second Battle of Khe Sanh.

The battle began on 20 January 1968, after the NVA had entrenched themselves between Hill 881 North and 881 South, and the 3rd Battalion dispatched two companies to drive

them out. On the next day NVA artillery shelled the base proper, destroying over 1500 tons of ammunition, and in the later stage capturing the town of Khe Sanh which lies off Highway 9. The Marines were now short of ammunition which had to be airlifted in. To further strengthen the garrison, Lieutenant Colonel John Mitchell's 1st Battalion, 9th Marines were brought in, as well as 318 men of the ARVN 37th Ranger Battalion and two 105mm howitzers. The greatest impediment facing the Marines was something that no one had any control over, except the Almighty – the monsoon rains. Nothing could move once the floods came and Highway 9 became completely waterlogged. Giap's strategy was simple, by-pass Khe Sanh and attack the populated cities. In spite of everything the American decision-makers did, that is exactly what Giap achieved.

On Tuesday, 30 January 1968, in one great co-ordinated surprise offensive, 60,000 enemy troops assaulted every important US installation, most

Men of E Company, 2nd Battalion, 3rd Marine Division struggle up Mutters Ridge north of Dong Ha.

of the cities, provincial and district capitals the entire length and breadth of the country. To make matters worse, Giap knew that the majority of ARVN troops responsible for defending the cities would be on leave for the Tet holiday. At 0247 hours Wednesday morning, a specially trained team of Viet Cong commandos fought their way into the US Embassy in Saigon. All four of the Army MPs on duty were killed at their posts. The only three Marines on duty in the Embassy building were Sergeant Ronald Harper, Sergeant Rudy Soto and Corporal George Zahuranic; the latter was wounded in the fighting. The Viet Cong commandos held the compound for over six hours before 12 of them were killed and the remaining two were captured. The siege of the Embassy was seen nation-wide by US citizens who until then had no real idea of what exactly was going on in Vietnam. This brought stark reality to their very doorsteps. The Presidential Palace in Saigon was attacked; the sprawling complex of the Tan Son Nhut Air Base was defended by a gallant unit of Air Force Security Police; and the Bien Hoa Air Base and Long Binh Army complex were hit by enemy sappers. In the north the situation was no better; all five provincial capitals were over-run. Thousands of political prisoners were set free from jails throughout the country as the Viet Cong ran riot everywhere. One major objective of Giap was to disrupt totally American air mobility and close air support. Da Nang, MAG-11, MAG-12 and MAG-13 at Chu Lai and MAG-16 at Marble

Marines on their way back to their operating base after gruelling fighting in the jungles in March 1966.

Mountain were subjected to stand-off artillery and rocket attacks on both the nights of 29 and 30 January, inflicting medium damage. Meanwhile, the North Vietnamese 2nd Division was approaching Da Nang city from the south and west, and was only stopped by the arrival of elements of the 1st Marine Division. Lieutenant General Cushman, in his command helicopter, spotted a further 200 enemy troops across the river south of base and advised Major General Robertson of the situation. Robertson immediately dispatched the 3rd Battalion, 5th Marines reinforced by the 2nd Battalion, 3rd Marines to eliminate this enemy concentration.

At Hue, the ancient imperial capital, NVA units infiltrated the city proper. The NVA forced the American and South Vietnamese troops to fight in the cities. American and ARVN forces drove the enemy out of the majority of the provincial capitals and major cities rapidly; however Hue presented much greater problems. It would take over a month before the city was secure again and this would be only after intense and bitter fighting from house to house, and street to street. The Marines in retaking Hue, lost 142 dead and 857 seriously wounded, and the imperial city was in ruins. The Marines were reinforced yet again. Colonel Adolph Schwenk's 27th Regimental Landing Team and the 3rd Brigade of the 82nd Airborne Division moved up to I Corps. Lieutenant General Cushman commanded the largest force ever led by a Marine (the only exception being Lieutenant General Roy Geiger's very brief command of the 10th Army on Okinawa after the sudden death of General Simon Buckner). To ensure smoother operational control, West-

moreland established a MACV advance command post at Phu Bai under General Creighton Abrams, a former Army Vice-Chief of Staff and, in addition, requested 206,000 men.

The net result of the Tet Offensive was 165,000 civilian dead, cities and towns in total ruin, and 15,000 NVA dead. The points which Giap hoped to make clear were (1) that despite an enormous US build up and some of the best military strategists in the business the NVA were able to mount an invasion of the south; (2) that massive bombing of the northern industrial targets and the cities of Hanoi and Haiphong had not appreciably weakened their will to fight; (3) that the NVA were not easily defeated in a major campaign although the US would have liked to believe that they were; (4) that a sense of hopelessness would spread throughout South Vietnam because the people no longer felt that the US could provide adequate protection for them; and (5) that this offensive totally undermined any support for the war that might have been growing in the USA – nothing was ever credible again concerning the war in Vietnam.

Back at Khe Sanh, the NVA were again advancing through the 20-foot high elephant grass. The complex was under constant ground, artillery, mortar and rocket attack from February through March. The cost of this static defense was 205 Marines killed and 1668 wounded in action, for the destruction of an estimated two divisions of NVA. Lieutenant General Cushman decided on the relief of Khe

Men of the 9th Marines and 12th Marines try to forget the war for a moment in January 1969.

Supersabres attack VC positions.

Sanh once the monsoon season was over. To coincide with this, he also planned to launch an attack into the DMZ and push an advance force through the A Shau valley in Thua Thien province. The 1st Air Cavalry Division with one ARVN battalion came in from the east and south, and the 1st Marines and a further three ARVN battalions moved west across Highway 9. A forward airstrip was set up at Ca Lu by the 6 April, and by the 12th, Highway 9 was open to traffic again. The 77-day long battle of Khe Sanh was over, on 14 April 1968, Easter Sunday. President Johnson awarded the 26th Marines the Presidential Unit Citation on 23 May for its gallant and courageous performance at Khe Sanh. Thus ended one of the most epic battles in which the US Marine Corps had ever been involved. At the end of 1968 Marine casualties were 4618 killed and 29,320 wounded in action.

Richard Nixon entered the White House in early 1969, and set into motion a change in policy. He had made a campaign promise that he would start withdrawing American troops once he took office. In Vietnam the US Forces kept up the pressure on the enemy while the politicians were fighting among themselves as to what the next course of action would be. The NVA on the other hand with nothing to lose and everything to gain launched a spring offensive on 1 April 1969. It was not as tremendous as the Tet of 1968 but it was a substantial countrywide offensive. On 1 April the following bases were hit by artillery fire:

Location	Time
Phan Rang	0023 hours
Pleiku	0105 hours
Nha Trang	0106 hours
Da Nang	0158 hours
Da Nang	0234 hours
Ban Me Thuot	0238 hours
Bien Hoa	0623 hours
Phan Rang	0935 hours

Also between 0001–0200 hours, 1 April 1969, the following locations were hit by enemy ground and artillery fire: Cau Mau, Soc Trang, Rac Gia, Tra Vinh, Moc Hoa, Vi Thanh, Ba Xoi, Binh Long, Vinh Long, Chi Lang and Ben Tre; in the IV Corps Tactical Zone alone there were 134 enemy-initiated actions.

On 8 May 1969 Nixon announced at Midway that the first contingent of US troops would be withdrawn from Vietnam by the end of August – 25,000 men. Despite these piecemeal withdrawals and the pressure put on the executive branch of the government by the peace movement, Americans continued to die in Vietnam for a further three years. But these were the final years of commitment to Vietnam by the Marines. By early 1970 the Marine Force in the country was gradually being reduced. This redeployment was really noticeable in the I Corps where for the first time the Army outnumbered the Marines. The Marines' final job was the defense of Da Nang and they were headquartered near Red Beach where the 9th Marines first came ashore back in 1965. By March 1972 when the enemy launched a major offensive at Easter there were only 500 Marines left in the country, from its peak of 85,755 men in 1968. A ceasefire was finally declared in January 1973. By the end of March the last American troop was out of the country. Thus ended the longest war in the 200-year history of our country.

Marine involvement in Southeast Asia was not over though, one more crisis loomed on the horizon. After the voluntary resignation of President Richard Nixon following the long and tortuous Watergate Scandal, Gerald Ford was sworn in as President of the United States. The Communists saw this as a heaven-sent opportunity to test American willpower after the evacuation of Saigon. A Cambodian gunboat stopped and forcefully seized an American, unarmed freighter, the *Mayaguez*, which had been steaming from Hong Kong to Sattahip, Thailand. President Ford immediately placed the 3rd Marine Division's 1100

Above: *A parachute jump from a North American OV-10A Bronco.*
Left: *South Vietnamese refugees are hurried off a CH-53 helicopter in 1975.*
Right above: *Safely aboard the USS* Hancock, *these were some of the 3000 people evacuated from Saigon in April 1975.*
Right: *The last stages of the war in 1975.*

man special landing team on alert, on Okinawa. All of this occurred on 12 and 13 May 1975. The Cambodians removed all the crew from the *Mayaguez* to an island in Kompong Som harbor called Kas Rong. Meanwhile, the 2nd Battalion, 9th Marines had flown in from Okinawa to U-Tapao Air Base, Thailand following an official protest from the Thai Government. On 15 May 227 Marines flew 195 miles in Air Force helicopters to retake the *Mayaguez* and free the American

26 March 1975
Hué falls to Communist forces

30 April 1975
Communist forces enter Saigon

COMMUNIST CONTROLLED AREAS
(APPROX), MID-JAN 1975
AND BY 25 MARCH

0   MILES   200
0   KILOMETERS .   300

188

Left: *Marine security guards escort South Vietnamese refugees in April 1975.*

merchant mariners that had been seized and imprisoned at Kas Rong. Under fighter cover, the Marines under Captain James Davis assaulted the island of Koh Tang where the *Mayaguez* was docked. The attack on Koh Tang was an error and wasted effort because the Marines had first priority to rescue the crew which had already been transferred to Kas Rong Island. The Cambodians shot down two of the approaching helicopters at 0615 hours. The first was brought down in flames; killing seven Marines, the Air Force co-pilot and two Navy corpsmen. Another three Marines were killed in the surf. The surviving members of this force swam out to sea and were later picked up by the guided-missile destroyer *Henry Wilson*. The second helicopter managed to land, but its crew and Marine detachment were cut off from help. After losing a further two helicopters, the rest of the attacking force was diverted to the western side of the island. The landing force came under intense Cambodian fire as they advanced. Unknown to the Marines at that time, the *Mayaguez* crew had been released two hours before the Marine attacks. After the initial mess with the crew safe on board the destroyer *Wilson*, the Marine assault was called off but there were still 225 Americans trapped on Koh Tang island. Helicopters and a boat from the *Wilson* managed to get in and evacuate the rest of the troops ashore, except for three Marines who were presumed dead. The total operation cost the US 41 dead (including 23 Air Force Security Policemen who died in a crash in Thailand) and 50 wounded. Altogether this made a grand total of 56,869 killed and 303,704 wounded in action in the Vietnam War.

Conclusion

On 10 November 1975 the Corps celebrated its 200th Birthday. In the past two hundred short years, the Marine Corps has made its indelible mark on the history of the United States of America. Individuals of outstanding caliber and leadership include Archibald Henderson, John Lejeune, John Trevett, Herman Hanneken, Christian Schilt, John Gamble, John Glenn (the astronaut), William Deane Hawkins ("the Hawk," the first man ashore at Tarawa), Dan Daly (the winner of two Medals of Honor) and "Chesty" Puller (winner of five Navy Crosses in battle).

Medal of honor winners – Vietnam

Name	Location	Date	Unit
Private First Class James Anderson	Cam Lo	1967	3rd Marines
Corporal Richard Anderson	Quang Tri	1969	3rd Recon Battalion
Private First Class Oscar Austin	Nr Da Nang	1969	7th Marines
Corporal Jedh Barker	Con Thien	1967	4th Marines
1st Lieutenant Harvey Barnum	Ky Phu	1965	9th Marines
2nd Lieutenant John Bobo	Quang Tri	1967	9th Marines
Private First Class Daniel Bruce	Quang Nam	1969	5th Marines
Private First Class Robert Burke	Le Nam	1968	27th Marines
Private First Class Bruce Carter	Quang Tri	1969	3rd Marines
Private First Class Raymond Clausen		1970	HMM-263
Staff Sergeant Peter Connor	Quang Ngai	1966	3rd Marines
Private First Class Ronald Coker	Quang Tri	1969	3rd Marines
Corporal Thomas Creek	Cam Lo	1969	9th Marines
Sergeant Rodney Davis	Quang Nam	1967	5th Marines
Corporal De La Garza	Nr Da Nang	1970	1st Marines
Private First Class Ralph Dias		1969	7th Marines
Private First Class Douglas Dickey	Gio Lanh	1967	4th Marines
Sergeant Paul Foster	Con Thien	1967	4th Marines
1st Lieutenant Wesley Fox	A Shau Valley	1969	9th Marines
Sergeant Alfredo Gonzalez	Hue	1968	1st Marines
Captain James Graham	Quang Tin	1967	5th Marines
2nd Lieutenant Terrance Graves	Quang Tri	1968	3rd Recon Battalion
Staff Sergeant Jimmie Howard	Chu Lai	1966	1st Recon Battalion
Corporal James Howe	Quang Nam	1970	7th Marines
Private First Class Robert Jenkins	FSB Argonne	1969	3rd Recon Battalion
Corporal Jose Jiminez	Que Son Valley	1969	7th Marines
Private First Class Ralph Johnson	Quan Duc Valley	1968	1st Recon Battalion
Corporal Miguel Keith	Quang Ngai	1970	CAP 1-2-3
Staff Sergeant Allan Kellogg	Quang Nam	1970	5th Marines
Captain Howard Lee	Cam Lo	1966	4th Marines
Captain James Livingston	Dai Do	1968	4th Marines
Private First Class Gary Martini	Que Son Valley	1967	1st Marines
Corporal Gary Maxam	Cam Lo	1968	4th Marines
Staff Sergeant John McGinty	Cam Lo	1966	4th Marines
Captain Robert Modrzejewski	Cam Lo	1966	4th Marines
Corporal William Morgan	Quang Tri	1969	9th Marines
Private First Class Melvin Newlin	Nong Son	1967	5th Marines
Corporal Thomas Noonan	A Shau Valley	1969	9th Marines
Corporal Robert O'Malley	Van Tuong Peninsula	1965	3rd Marines
Corporal Joe Paul	Chu Lai	1965	4th Marines
Corporal William Perkins	Quang Tri	1967	3rd Marine Division
Sergeant Lawrence Peters	Quang Tin	1967	5th Marines
Private First Class Jimmy Phipps	An Hoa	1969	1st Engineer Battalion
Corporal Richard Pittman	Nr DMZ	1966	5th Marines
Captain Stephen Pless	Quang Ngai	1967	VMO-6
Corporal William Prom	An Hoa	1969	3rd Marines
1st Lieutenant Frank Reasoner	Da Nang	1965	3rd Recon Battalion
Sergeant Walter Singleton	Gio Linh	1967	9th Marines
Corporal Larry Smedley	Quang Nam	1967	7th Marines
Staff Sergeant Karl Taylor	Nr Da Nang	1968	26th Marines
Captain Sando Vargas	Dai Do	1968	4th Marines
Corporal Lester Weber	Quang Nam	1968	7th Marines
Corporal Roy Wheat	Quang Nam	1967	7th Marines
Private First Class Dewayne Williams	Quang Nam	1968	1st Marines
Private First Class Alfred Wilson	Quang Tri	1969	9th Marines
Corporal Kenneth Worley	Quang Nam	1968	7th Marines

Total: 56

Above: *USAF security police and ARVN personnel search for Viet Cong guerrillas on the perimeter of the Tan Son Nhut air base during Tet.*
Left: *Bombs destined for use by B-52s over North Vietnam are transported from Guam to Vietnam.*
Below left: *Smoke rises from a fuel dump hit by a Viet Cong mortar attack on Khe Sanh. The battle for this Marine fire-support base did not take place until March–April 1968.*
Below: *Air support for I Company, 3rd Marine Division arrives after six Viet Cong tried to penetrate their defenses south of Da Nang.*

INDEX

ACKNOWLEDGMENTS

Syd and Charlotte Mayer, two of my closest friends.
Special thanks for the help of Frank Papasadora, US Marine Corps Eastcote, London, England.
US Marine Corps Historical and Museum Division.
British Imperial War Museum.
Royal Institute of International Affairs.
International Institute of Strategic Studies.
New York Public Library.
Yonkers, New York, Public Library.

Bison Picture Library: p 57 (bottom), 61, 63 (top), 66, 67, 68, (center), 70–71, 74–75, 80 (top), 86–87, 88–89, 126–127.
Library of Congress: p 24–25, 26.

US Marine Corps Gazette.
London Borough of Hillingdon Libraries.

The author would like to thank Richard Natkiel who prepared the maps and Mike Badrocke who supplied the technical illustrations.

Bison Books would like to thank the US Marine Corps Headquarters which provided most of the pictures used in this book. All the other pictures were supplied by the following picture libraries:

National Archives: p 22 (top), 23 (top), 56, 62 (top), 62–63, 64, 68 (top), 68–69, 72–73, 73 (top), 76 (both), 78–79, 80 (bottom), 81, 82, (bottom), 84–85, 85 (bottom), 86

(top), 87 (top), 105 (top), 125 (top right).
US Navy: p 16–17 (both), 22–23, 57 (top), 58–59, 60 (both), 65, 72–73 (top), 86 (center), 119 (top), 137 (top).